BETTER
COOKING LIBRARY

PIE
COOK BOOK

 OTTENHEIMER PUBLISHERS, INC., OWINGS MILLS, MD. 21117

Cover photograph by General Foods Inc.

Decorative Art by Ella George

CONTENTS

Pie Cook Book

By and large, the favorite dessert of the majority of American men is Apple Pie. Therefore it behooves every American female to know how to bake an apple pie to perfection—and this is the book to show her how. It will unlock the secret, not only for a good apple pie, but many, many other kinds of pie.

The secret of success for any pie is the crust. Step-by-step pictures show how to make a basic flaky pie crust, using shortening. It shows how to make a pie shell, how to make a double crust pie and how to seal and flute the edges. We also have step-by-step photos on an oil pastry, that is as simple as 1-2-3. And of course we have included graham cracker crusts, cookie crusts and how to make a meringue shell.

As for the fillings, they come in all the fruit flavors, either plain or with cream or chiffon base. Try mixing fruits in a pie, or try something new, such as a pear pie. Chiffon pies, that come in all the colors of the rainbow, are usually a favorite with the ladies.

Pastry

Pastry should be flaky, tender and delicate; it should not crumble when broken but shatter in layers. Use light touch in mixing and rolling.

Chocolate Coconut Pie Crust

2 squares unsweetened chocolate

2 tablespoons butter

2 tablespoons hot milk or water

⅔ cup sifted confectioners' sugar

1½ cups shredded coconut

Melt chocolate and butter in top of a double boiler, stirring until blended. Combine milk and sugar. Add to chocolate mixture, stirring well. Add coconut and mix well. Spread on bottom and sides of greased 9-inch pie plate. Chill until firm. To serve fill crust with ice cream, pudding mix or parfait filling. Makes one 9-inch pie shell.

Baker's Unsweetened Chocolate

TENDER PASTRY

Starting with the picture at the left, the next fourteen photos show you how to make tender pastry. This complete how-to recipe makes one two-crust nine-inch pie or two nine-inch pie shells. To start with, sift 2 cups of flour and 1¼ teaspoons of salt into a bowl. Measure out ⅔ cup of shortening.

With a pastry blender, cut in ⅓ cup of the shortening until mixture is consistency of cornmeal. Cut in second ⅓ cup until mixture is size of small peas.

As shown at left, sprinkle ¼ cup icy cold water, one tablespoonful at a time, over mixture. Toss lightly with a fork to make mixture hold together.

Turn mixture out onto a piece of waxed paper, press gently with hands into ball shape, chill for a while.

Divide ball of dough in half. On a lightly-floured board, roll dough into a circle about ⅛ inch thick. Roll lightly · from center, lift near edges.

Now fold dough in half (see above), then lift gently and lay fold line across center of pan. Carefully, now, unfold the dough in pan to original circle.

Fit pastry into pan by lifting and patting gently. The thing to remember here is: do not stretch it to make it fit. If you do it will shrink when baked.

In order to have enough pastry dough to work with when fluting the edges (see next photo) trim edges (above) leaving ½ inch beyond plate.

Fold edges of crust under so that it stands up. Flute edges by pressing index finger of one hand between thumb and index finger of other hand.

Prick pastry all over with a fork to allow steam to escape and bake in a very hot oven (450°) 12 to 15 minutes, or until crust is lightly browned.

For a two-crust pie, roll half of pastry and fit into pan for a single crust. Fill. Trim even with plate. Remaining half is slashed with pattern.

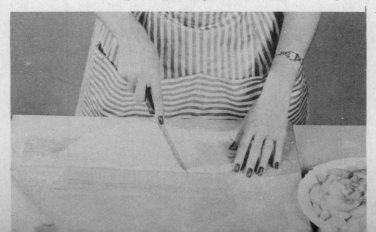

After cutting slits, moisten lower edges of top pastry with water, place on filling and unfold. Pat edges together, trim ½ inch over, tuck under.

Seal crust (below) by pressing at an angle with thumb and bent index finger. Or, use any other kind of edge desired. Bake according to recipe.

Flaky Pastry

2 cups sifted flour	⅔ cup shortening
1 teaspoon salt	⅓ cup milk

Mix together flour and salt. Cut in shortening with a pastry blender or 2 knives until mixture looks like coarse cornmeal. Remove ¼ cup of this mixture. Mix well with the milk and stir into the flour shortening mixture until a dough is formed. Press into a ball and flatten slightly. Roll half the dough between 2 pieces of waxed paper as shown on page **16** for Salad Oil Pastry. Proceed according to directions for either pie shells or a double crust pie. Makes two 8 or 9-inch shells or one double crust pie.

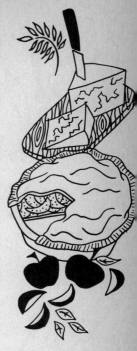

Spicy Pastry

2 cup sifted flour	¼ teaspoon ginger
¼ teaspoon baking soda	¼ teaspoon cloves
¼ cup sugar	⅔ cup shortening
1 teaspoon salt	1 tablespoon vinegar
½ teaspoon cinnamon	3 tablespoons orange juice

Sift together dry ingredients. Cut in ⅓ cup of the shortening to the consistency of cornmeal. Cut in remaining ⅓ cup of the shortening to the consistency of peas. Mix together vinegar and orange juice. Add slowly to dry ingredients, mixing lightly with a fork. Turn onto a piece of waxed paper and shape into a ball. Chill. Roll out dough on a lightly floured board according to picture directions. Makes one 9-inch 2 crust pie or two 9-inch pie shells.

Quick Coconut Crust

2 tablespoons soft butter	1 package (1½ cups) shredded coconut

Spread butter evenly in an 8 or 9-inch pie plate. Sprinkle coconut in pan, pressing gently into butter on bottom and sides. Bake in a slow oven (300° F) 15 to 20 minutes. Cool crust before filling. Makes one 8 or 9-inch shell.

GRAHAM CRACKER
PIE CRUST

To make the graham cracker pie crust shown, place twenty graham crackers in a plastic or cellophane bag, roll into fine crumbs. Pour crumbs into a bowl, add one-quarter cup of sugar and one-quarter cup of softened butter. Mix ingredients with blender.

Pour crumb mixture into a nine-inch pie plate. Set an eight-inch pie plate on top of crumbs and press them firmly into an even layer against bottom and sides of pan. Bake in moderately hot oven (375°F) for eight minutes. Take out and cool before filling.

To make a lattice-top pie crust, use half of the pastry for bottom shell, roll second half into twelve-inch circle, cut into one-half inch strips with a pastry wheel or sharp knife. Lay four or five strips loosely across top of filling as shown in above photograph. Now see photo below.

Take remaining strips and, in basket-weave fashion, complete lattice-top design. Trim even with plate edge, moisten with water, press down.

SALAD OIL PASTRY

Sift together into a bowl two cups of flour and one teaspoon of salt, combine one-half cup salad oil and one-quarter cup milk in a measuring cup.

Pour salad oil and milk mixture (all at once) over flour. These and the next five photos comprise Salad Oil how-to picture-recipe set.

Stir and mix lightly with a fork (above) until flour is entirely moistened.

Now we are ready for rolling. Round up dough into ball, divide in halves.

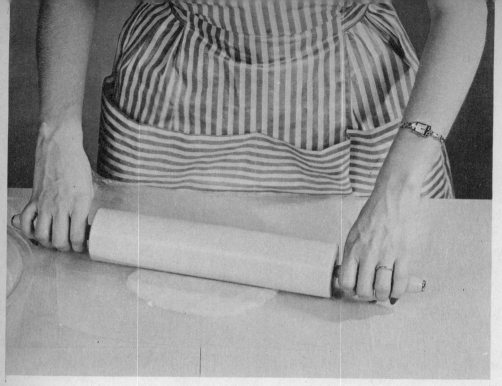

Place half of dough between two squares of waxed paper. Wipe table with a damp cloth to keep paper from slipping while rolling. Roll dough lightly from center until circle reaches edges of waxed paper.

Remove top sheet of waxed paper. Lift paper and pastry by top corners and place paper-side up over pie pan. Peel off paper, ease into pan.

Trim bottom crust even with sides of pan. Fill. Roll out remaining dough and repeat process. Invert over filling and peel off paper.

Quick Oatmeal Pie Crust

2 cups quick oats
⅓ cup melted butter or margarine
¼ teaspoon salt

2 teaspoons grated lemon rind
3 tablespoons light corn syrup

Combine quick oats and melted butter and stir well. Add salt, lemon rind and corn syrup. With the back of a spoon press mixture lightly into a pie plate. Bake in a moderately hot oven (375° F) 15 to 20 minutes or until lightly browned. Cool before filling. Makes one 8 or 9-inch pie crust.

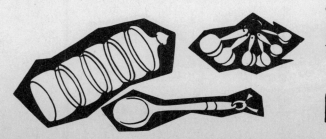

Margarine Pie Crust

½ cup margarine
¼ cup boiling water
1½ cups sifted flour
¼ teaspoon salt

Cream margarine until soft and light. Add boiling water and mix thoroughly. Cool. Combine flour and salt and add to margarine mixture, stirring lightly with a fork. Wrap dough in waxed paper and chill. Roll out on a lightly floured board. Fit according to directions on page 9. For a baked shell follow directions for baking. Otherwise fill and bake according to directions in recipe. Makes one 9-inch shell.

Chocolate Cookie Crumb Crust

1¼ cups finely crushed
   chocolate cookies
½ cup sugar
¼ cup softened butter or
   margarine

Combine all ingredients and mix thoroughly. Press evenly around bottom and sides of pie plate. Fill with desired filling and chill well before serving. Makes one 9-inch pie crust.

Bran Pie-Crust Shells

⅓ cup bran
2 cups sifted flour
½ teaspoon salt
⅔ cup shortening
6 tablespoons cold water,
   about

Crush bran into fine crumbs; mix with flour and salt. Cut in ⅓ cup of the shortening to the consistency of cornmeal. Cut in remaining shortening to the consistency of peas. Sprinkle cold water over top a little at a time, mixing with a fork until dough is just moist enough to hold together. Turn onto a piece of waxed paper and shape into a ball. Roll out according to directions on page 7. Makes two 8 or 9-inch pie shells or four 4-inch tart shells.

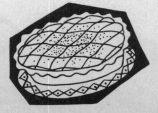

Macaroon Pie Crust

1 egg white
2 tablespoons sugar
1 tablespoon light corn syrup

½ teaspoon vanilla
2 cups coconut, finely chopped

Beat egg whites until foamy. Add sugar and beat until mixture will stand in soft peaks. Add corn syrup and flavoring. Fold in coconut. Using the back of a spoon, press macaroon mixture firmly on bottom and sides of a well-buttered 9-inch pie plate. Bake in a moderate oven (350° F) 15 minutes, or until lightly browned. Cool before using. Makes one 9-inch shell.

Gingersnap Pie Crust

20 gingersnaps
3 tablespoons sugar
½ teaspoon cinnamon

½ cup softened butter or margarine

Crush gingersnaps with a rolling pin; measure out 1¼ cups. Place in a bowl and add sugar and cinnamon. Blend in softened butter with a fork and mix well. Press crumb mixture with the back of a spoon into a 9-inch pie plate. Bake crust in a moderate oven (350° F) 10 minutes. Cool before filling. Good with pumpkin chiffon mixture. Makes one 9-inch pie shell.

Brazil Nut Pie Crust

1½ cups ground Brazil nuts
   (¾ pound unshelled nuts)

3 tablespoons sugar

Mix nuts and sugar in a 10-inch pie plate. Press mixture with the back of a tablespoon against the bottom and sides of pie plate. Crust is ready for filling now or it can be baked before filling. If a toasted flavor is desired, bake in a hot oven (400° F) 8 minutes or until lightly browned. Chill before filling. Makes one 10-inch shell.

1-2-3 Pastry

Single Crust Pie	Double Crust Pie
1⅓ cups sifted flour	2 cups sifted flour
½ teaspoon salt	1 teaspoon salt
⅓ cup corn oil	½ cup corn oil
2 tablespoons cold water	3 tablespoons cold water

Combine flour and salt in mixing bowl. Blend in corn oil, mixing thoroughly with fork. Sprinkle all water on top; mix well. Press firmly into ball with hands. (If slightly dry, mix in 1 to 2 tablespoons additional corn oil.)

Single Crust: Flatten dough slightly, and immediately roll out to 12 inch circle between 2 pieces of waxed paper. (Wipe table with damp cloth to keep paper from slipping.) Peel off top paper; place pastry circle in 9-inch pie pan, paper side up. Peel off paper; fit pastry loosely into pan. Trim pastry ½ inch beyond rim of pan, if necessary. Flute edge. If shell is to be baked before filling, prick thoroughly and bake in hot oven (450°F.) until golden brown, 12 to 15 minutes. If shell and filling are to be baked together, do not prick shell; bake pie according to filling used.

Double Crust: Divide dough almost in half. Flatten larger portion slightly; roll out and place in pie pan as directed above. Fill as desired. Trim pastry, if necessary. Roll out remaining pastry for top crust. Peel off paper, cut slits in pastry to permit steam to escape during baking, and place over filling. Trim ½ inch beyond rim of pan. Fold edges of both crusts under; seal and flute. Bake pie according to filling used.

Note: If unsifted flour is used, measure 1 cup plus 2 tablespoons flour for single crust, and 1¾ cups for double crust. To measure, dip dry nested measuring cups and measuring spoons (as needed) into flour; level off with straight edged spatula.

PASTRY VARIATIONS
(for single crust pie)

Lemon Pastry: Follow recipe for 1-2-3 Pastry, stirring in ½ teaspoon grated lemon rind with flour and salt and substituting lemon juice for water.

Cheddar Cheese Pastry: Follow recipe for 1-2-3 Pastry, adding ½ cup finely shredded Cheddar cheese to flour and salt.

Nut Pastry: Follow recipe for 1-2-3 Pastry, adding ¼ cup finely chopped nuts to flour and salt.

Cream Cheese Pastry: Follow recipe for 1-2-3 Pastry, cutting 3 ounces cream cheese into flour and salt with pastry blender or 2 knives.

Chocolate Pastry: Follow recipe for 1-2-3 Pastry sifting ¼ cup cocoa and 1 tablespoon sugar with flour and salt.

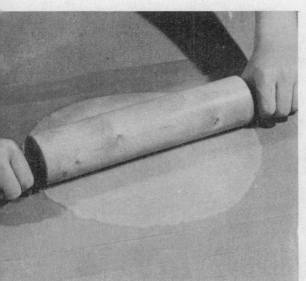

Mix together flour and salt. Pour in corn oil; blend with a fork.

Sprinkle all of water over mixture. Mix well. Press dough firmly into a ball with hands.

Roll dough out between 2 sheets of waxed paper. To keep paper from slipping, wipe table top with a damp cloth.

After removing top sheet of waxed paper, use bottom sheet of paper to lift crust, carefully placed rolled pie crust over pie pan.

Remove waxed paper and fit pastry carefully into pan.

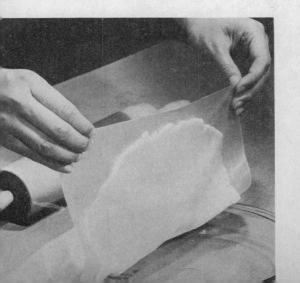

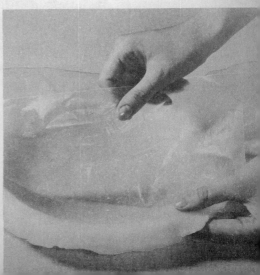

Coconut Macaroon Crust

1 egg white
2 tablespoons sugar
1 tablespoon light corn
  syrup
½ teaspoon vanilla or ¼
  teaspoon almond extract

2 cups flaked coconut
1 quart vanilla or
  peppermint ice cream
Chocolate sauce

Beat egg white until foamy. Add sugar and beat until mixture will stand in soft peaks. Add corn syrup and flavoring. Fold in coconut. Using the back of a fork, press macaroon mixture firmly on bottom and sides of well-buttered 9-inch pie pan. Bake in moderate oven (350°F.) for 15 minutes, or until lightly browned. Cool. To serve, fill cold crust with ice cream and pass Chocolate Sauce.

Chocolate Sauce

1 package (4 ounces)
  sweet cooking chocolate
2 tablespoons water

3 tablespoons cream or
  evaporated milk

Combine chocolate and water in saucepan. Place over low heat and stir constantly until chocolate is melted—about 3 to 5 minutes. Remove from heat. Add cream and stir until smooth. Serve warm or cold. Makes ¾ cup sauce.

Baker's Angel Flake Coconut

Spicy Walnut Meringue Shell

½ cup toasted walnuts
3 egg whites
¼ teaspoon cream of tartar
⅛ teaspoon salt
1 cup sugar
½ teaspoon cinnamon

Chop walnuts fine. Beat egg whites with cream of tartar and salt, in a medium sized bowl, to soft peaks. Gradually beat in sugar, about 2 tablespoons at a time, until meringue stands up in stiff glossy peaks. Beat in cinnamon along with the last ¼ cup sugar. Gently fold in walnuts. Pile meringue in a lightly greased 9 or 10-inch pie plate. Spread over bottom and up sides to form crust. Bottom of shell should be about ¼-inch thick, sides about 1-inch thick. Bake in a slow oven (275°F.) 50 to 60 minutes or until a very light tan in color. Turn off oven and leave meringue to cool with door closed. Meringue will crack and fall in center while cooling. Makes 1 large shell.

Mayonnaise Pie Crust

1 cup sifted flour
¼ teaspoon salt
⅓ cup mayonnaise
1½ tablespoons water
½ teaspoon grated lemon rind

Mix flour and salt. Stir in mayonnaise with a fork. Add water and rind and mix well. Roll dough out on a lightly floured board to a 12-inch circle. Fit lightly into a 9-inch pie plate. Flute edges. Or divide dough into 6 portions and roll each into a circle. Fit into individual pie plates and flute edges. Makes one 9-inch shell or 6 tart shells.

Cornflake Pie Crust

4 cups cornflakes
¼ cup sugar
½ cup softened butter or margarine

Place cornflakes in a paper bag and crush fine with a rolling pin. Pour into a bowl (there should be about 1 cup of crushed cornflakes). Add sugar. Blend in the softened butter, mixing well. With the back of a spoon, press mixture into an 8-inch pie plate. Chill thoroughly. If desired, bake crust in a moderate oven (350° F) about 10 minutes. Chill well before filling. Makes one 8-inch pie crust.

LOVELY MERINGUE

Start with two or three egg whites, according to the recipe you are using. Be sure whites are at room temperature for greatest volume. Beat until frothy.

Add sugar gradually, one tablespoon at a time (two tablespoons to each egg white), beating well after each addition, until egg whites stand in stiff peaks.

Spoon mounds of meringue around edges of the filling, making sure to touch crust all around, heap the remaining meringue inside as shown.

Meringue Pie Crust

2 egg whites
¼ teaspoon salt

¼ teaspoon cream of tartar
½ cup sugar

Beat egg whites until frothy; add salt and cream of tartar and beat until stiff but not dry. Gradually add sugar and beat until meringue stands in stiff peaks and is smooth and glossy. Spread in bottom and sides of a well greased 9-inch pie plate. Bake in a slow oven (250° F) about 1 hour or until lightly browned. Fill with berries or ice cream just before serving. Makes one 9-inch shell.

Pull up points of meringue with back of spoon, bake in hot oven (400°F) five to ten minutes until delicately browned. Cool away from drafts.

Tarts

Here are tarts that will steal the hearts of your family—and you'll be crowned Queen of the Day!

Fresh Cherry Tarts

½ cup sugar
¼ cup cornstarch
¼ teaspoon salt
½ cup light corn syrup

3 cups fresh, sour cherries, pitted
¼ teaspoon almond extract
6 3½-inch baked tart shells

Combine sugar, cornstarch and salt in top of a double boiler. Add corn syrup and mix well. Add cherries. Place over boiling water and cook, stirring frequently, until mixture thickens. Cover and continue cooking about 20 minutes, stirring occasionally. Remove from heat and add almond extract. Cool. Pour into baked tart shells and chill. Serve with whipped cream, if desired. Makes 6 tarts.

Roll out pastry to ⅛-inch thickness and cut into 4-inch squares with a pastry wheel or sharp knife. Next place not more than a tablespoon of mincemeat or other filling in the corner of each square.

Fruit Turnovers

1 recipe pastry	½ cup brown sugar
1 No. 2 can sliced peaches, well drained	½ teaspoon ginger

Roll out pastry ⅛ inch thick. Cut in 8 rounds 6 inches across. Place 3 peach slices on half of each circle. Sprinkle with sugar and ginger. Moisten edge of pastry with water; fold over and press edges together with a fork. Prick tops with a fork. Bake in a moderately hot oven (400° F) 30 minutes. Makes 8 turnovers.

Moisten edges of turnovers with water and fold over dough from one corner to the other. Seal edges of each by pressing with a fork. Prick tops and bake in a very hot oven (450° F) for about 15 minutes.

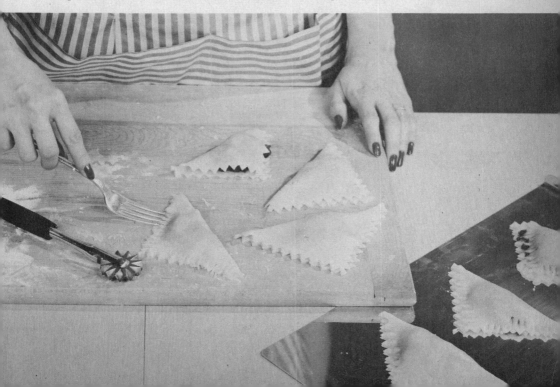

1-2-3 Tart Shells

1⅓ cups sifted flour
½ teaspoon salt

⅓ cup corn oil
2 tablespoon cold water

Combine flour and salt in a mixing bowl. Blend in corn oil, mixing thoroughly with a fork. Sprinkle all water on top; mix well. Press firmly into ball with hands. (If slightly dry, mix in 1 to 2 tablespoons additional corn oil.) Place ball of dough on a piece of heavy duty aluminum foil about 15 inches long. Flatten ball slightly and cover with waxed paper. Roll out dough to a 12-inch square. Remove waxed paper. Mark off dough into desired shapes with edge of knife. (Makes 4-inch squares or circles, or triangles 4-inches long on each side.) Cut through dough and foil with scissors. Turn up sides of dough and foil, about 1-inch all around. Pinch corners, or flute circles, to hold in place. Prick and place on ungreased baking sheet. Bake in a very hot oven (450°F.) until shells are golden brown, 12 to 15 minutes. Cool. Remove foil. Fill shells as desired. Makes 9 squares or circles, or 15 triangles.

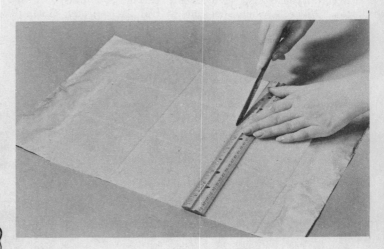

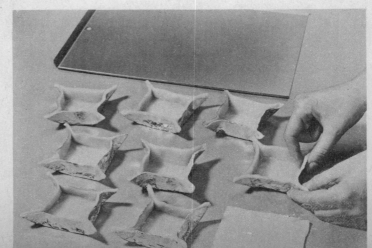

Lunch Box Turnovers

1 recipe pastry	1 tablespoon cornstarch
⅔ cup cooked prunes	¼ teaspoon salt
⅓ cup cooked apricots	1 tablespoon lemon juice
¼ cup sugar	

Roll out pastry ⅛-inch thick. Cut into twelve 4-inch squares. Combine remaining ingredients in a saucepan and cook over low heat about 5 minutes. Place 1½ tablespoons of the filling on half of each square; fold pastry over to form a triangle. Seal edges and flute with fingers or a fork. Prick holes in top with a fork. Bake in a hot oven (425° F) about 15 minutes or until lightly browned. Makes 12 turnovers.

Tom Thumb Tarts

Pastry

1 cup butter or margarine	2 cups sifted flour
2 packages (3-ounces) cream cheese	

Soften butter at room temperature. Add cream cheese; beat until smooth and creamy. Add flour ½ cup at a time, blending well after each addition. Work with fingers to a smooth dough. Shape into balls about ½" in diameter. Place each ball in cup of small muffin pans; press with thumb to line bottom and sides easily.

Filling

2 eggs	2 tablespoons melted
1½ cups brown sugar	butter or margaine
1 tablespoon instant coffee	1 teaspoon vanilla
Dash of salt	¾ cup coarsely broken pecans

Beat eggs with fork just enough to blend yolks and whites. Combine sugar, instant coffee and salt; add gradually to eggs, beating well after each addition. Add melted butter and vanilla. Sprinkle pecans in pastry cup; spoon filling over pecans, filling cups not quite to tops. Bake in moderate oven (350°F.), 20 minutes or until set. Makes about two dozen.

Pan American Coffee Bureau

Processed Apples Institute, Inc.

Individual Apple Sauce-Date Pies

1 ½ cups sifted all-purpose
  flour
¼ teaspoon salt
½ cup shortening
½ cup grated American
  cheese
3 tablespoons cold water
2 cups canned apple sauce

1 cup chopped pitted dates
⅓ cup brown sugar
½ teaspoon nutmeg
1 ½ teaspoons grated lemon
  rind

Sift together flour and salt. Cut in shortening with 2 knives or pastry blender. Add cheese; mix well. Add enough water to hold ingredients together. Chill. (Or use your favorite pastry mix and add the grated cheese.) Combine apple sauce, dates, brown sugar, nutmeg and lemon rind; mix well. Line individual pie plates with pastry, reserving enough for tops. Place an equal amount of apple sauce mixture into pie plates. Moisten edges of pastry with cold water. Roll out remaining pastry; cover tops of pies. Press edges with tines of fork; trim pastry to edge of pie plate. Prick tops to allow steam to escape. Bake in hot oven (400°F.) 30 minutes. Makes six 4-inch individual pies, or one 9-inch pie.

Apple Blossom Tarts

Pastry for one crust pie
½ cup sugar
3 tablespoons cinnamon
   drop candies
¾ cup warm water
Dash of salt

2-3 apples
24 tiny marshmallows
4 tablespoons broken
   walnut meats
2 tablespoons crushed
   peppermint stick candy

Roll out pastry. Cut rounds to fit bottom of custard cups. Invert 4 custard cups on a cookie sheet. Place one round of pastry on the bottom of each cup, then overlap 4 or 5 rounds for "petal" sides, moistening the rounds where they overlap. Prick well with fork, bake in very hot oven (450°F.) for 15 minutes or until browned. Cool.

Combine sugar, cinnamon candies, water and salt in a saucepan. Simmer until candies are completely dissolved. Peel, quarter and core apples; then cut quarters into thick half-slices. Add apples to syrup gradually so that the temperature of the syrup is not reduced sharply. Simmer apples, turning and basting with the syrup, until *barely tender*. Lift apples from syrup and spread out on platter to cool. Boil down syrup until it falls heavily from a spoon. Cool. Toss cinnamon apple chunks, marshmallows, walnuts and peppermint candy together, lightly, adding syrup as desired. Fill pastry cups. Serve, chilled, with a dollop of whipped cream, tinted apple green, if you wish.

Washington State Apple Commission

Nut Cookie Tarts

⅓ cup sifted flour
¼ teaspoon salt
¼ teaspoon baking soda
1½ cups quick-cooking oats
3 tablespoons finely chopped nuts
¼ cup margarine

¼ cup granulated sugar
¼ cup brown sugar
1 egg
½ teaspoon vanilla
¼ teaspoon maple flavor
Mixed fruits
Whipped cream

Sift together flour, salt and soda. Stir in oats and nuts. Cream margarine well. Add sugars and blend well. Add egg and flavorings and beat well. Add dry ingredients and blend well. Divide dough into 6 individual greased pie pans and press in dough to the thickness of pie crust. Bake in a moderate oven (350°F.) 20 to 25 minutes. After about 10 minutes of baking time it may be necessary to press down dough in the pans again. Cool. Fill with any desired combination of cooked or fresh fruit. Top with whipped cream. Makes 6 servings.

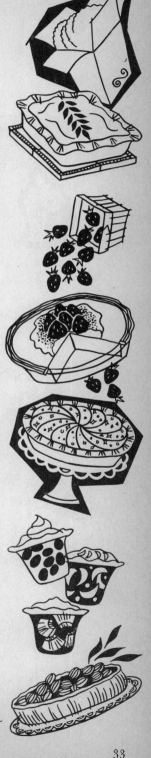

French Glaze Cherry Tart

1 cup sifted flour
½ teaspoon salt
⅓ cup shortening

2 tablespoons milk
2 tablespoons butter

Sift together flour and salt. With a pastry blender or 2 knives, cut in the shortening. Sprinkle milk over mixture, tossing with a fork until dough stays together. Round up into a ball and roll out on a lightly floured board to ⅛-inch thickness. Dot with butter. Fold so that the two sides meet in the center and seal by pressing the side edge of pastry with fingers. Fold ends to center and seal. Roll dough out again into a circle 1½ inches larger than 9-inch pie pan. Place in pie pan. Fold edge under and flute to make a stand-up collar. Prick thoroughly with a fork. Bake in a very hot oven (475°F.) 8 to 10 minutes. Cool.

1 3-ounce package cream cheese
4 cups sweet cherries, pitted
1 cup water

⅔ cup sugar
2⅔ tablespoons cornstarch
1 tablespoon lemon juice
Sweetened whipped cream

Mash cream cheese and stir until smooth. Spread over bottom of pie shell. Cover cheese with 2 cups of the cherries. Combine remaining cherries and water and boil 5 minutes. Stir in combined sugar and cornstarch. Boil 1 minute, stirring constantly. Remove from heat. Blend in lemon juice. Cool and pour over cherries in pie shell. Just before serving decorate with whipped cream. Makes one 9-inch pie.

Chess Pies

½ cup butter or margarine
1 teaspoon vanilla
1 cup sugar
1 egg white
3 egg yolks, beaten

1 cup chopped raisins
1 cup chopped nuts
10 unbaked tart shells in
    2¾-inch muffin pans

Cream butter and vanilla. Gradually beat in sugar until light and fluffy. Beat egg white until stiff and fold into beaten egg yolks. Blend well into sugar mixture. Add raisins and nuts. Pour into tart shells. Bake in a hot oven (400° F) 25 minutes. Serve topped with whipped cream, if desired. Makes 10 tarts.

Meringue Tart Shells

4 egg whites   1 cup sugar

Beat egg whites until foamy. Beat sugar in gradually, 1 tablespoon at a time, beating thoroughly after each addition. Continue beating until meringue forms sharp peaks when beater is raised. Shape meringue into nests with a spoon or pastry bag on brown paper on a baking sheet. Bake in a very slow oven (250° F) 1 hour and 20 minutes until shells are dried and the tops are cream colored. Remove from paper as soon as baked. Cool completely before serving. Fill with fruit or ice cream for serving. Makes 12 shells.

Pumpkin Marmalade Tarts

¾ cup strained cooked
    or canned pumpkin
⅓ cup firmly packed
    brown sugar
½ teaspoon cinnamon
¼ teaspoon ginger
¼ teaspoon nutmeg
½ teaspoon salt

2 egg yolks, beaten
¾ cup milk
¼ cup evaporated milk
6 unbaked tart shells
3 tablespoons orange
    marmalade
2 egg whites
4 tablespoons sugar

Combine pumpkin, brown sugar, spices and salt. Stir in egg yolks, milk and evaporated milk. Pour mixture into unbaked tart shells. Bake in a hot oven (450° F) 15 minutes; reduce temperature to 325° F and continue baking about 20 minutes or until set. Spread tarts with orange marmalade. Beat egg whites until stiff. Gradually beat in sugar and continue beating until well mixed. Spread over top of marmalade. Bake in a hot oven (425° F) about 5 minutes, or until lightly browned. Makes 6 tarts.

Pear Squares

2 to 3 fresh pears
Pie pastry (using 3 cups
    flour)
½ cup sugar
1 tablespoon butter
1 cup water

1½ cups brown sugar
1 tablespoon lemon juice
1 tablespoon butter
1 stick cinnamon, broken
Pinch of salt

Wash, peel and core pears. Save peelings in saucepan.
Make pastry using 3 cups of flour. Chill, then roll out into
rectangle. Cut into strips, 4 x 8 inches. Slice pears and place
on half of each pastry strip. Sprinkle pears with sugar, dot
with butter. Fold pastry over and seal edges with tines of
fork. Cut slits or pear shape on top of pastry. Bake on baking sheet in hot oven (425°F.) for 20 minutes or until
golden brown. Serve warm with Cinnamon Sauce.

Cinnamon Sauce: Boil pear peelings with 1 cup water for
5 minutes. Strain and discard peelings. Add brown sugar,
lemon juice, butter, cinnamon and salt to water in which
pear peelings cooked. Bring to boil and simmer for 5 to 6
minutes. Strain out cinnamon stick pieces. Serve warm.

Corn Products Company

Quick Lemon Meringue Tarts

1 package lemon pudding or pie mix	2 eggs, separated
½ cup sugar	6 large or 12 small baked tart shells
2½ cups water	¼ cup sugar

Combine lemon pudding, sugar and water in a saucepan. Beat yolks slightly and add to mixture. Cook over medium heat, stirring constantly, until mixture thickens and comes to a boil. Cool slightly. Pour into baked tart shells. Beat egg whites until stiff but not dry; gradually beat in sugar until mixture stands in peaks. Pile lightly on tarts. Bake in a hot oven (425° F) about 5 minutes until lightly browned. Makes 6 large or 12 small tarts.

Lemon Cheese Tart

1 cup sifted flour
½ teaspoon salt
⅓ cup shortening
3 to 4 tablespoons cold water
1 8-ounce package cream cheese

2 eggs
½ cup sugar
1 teaspoon vanilla
1 teaspoon grated lemon rind
1 tablespoon lemon juice
½ cup heavy cream

Sift together the flour and salt. Cut in shortening until particles are the size of small peas. Sprinkle cold water gradually over mixture, tossing lightly with a fork until dough is moist enough to hold together. Form into a ball. Roll out on a lightly floured board into a circle 1½ inches larger than an 8-inch pie pan. Fit pastry loosely into pie pan. Fold edge to form a standing rim; flute edge. Prick crust with a fork. Bake in a hot oven (425°F.) 8 to 10 minutes. Soften cream cheese and whip until fluffy. Add eggs, one at a time, beating well after each addition. Blend in sugar, vanilla, lemon rind and lemon juice. Mix well. Turn into baked pie shell. Bake in a moderate oven (350°F.) 15 to 20 minutes until slightly firm. Cool. Chill at least 1 hour before serving. Whip cream until stiff. Flavor to taste. Spread over pie before serving. Garnish with grated lemon rind. Makes one 8-inch pie.

French Strawberry Cream Tart

1½ cups sifted flour
½ teaspoon baking powder
¼ teaspoon salt

½ cup butter
1 egg
½ cup sugar

Sift together flour, baking powder and salt. Cut in butter until it is the consistency of corn meal. Beat egg slightly, add sugar and beat until just blended. Stir into flour mixture and mix well. Place dough in a greased 9-inch pie pan and press it out so that it covers bottom and sides of pan. Bake in a hot oven (425°F.) about 20 minutes. When cool, fill with the following custard mixture.

⅔ cup sugar
4 tablespoons cornstarch
¼ teaspoon salt
2 cups milk

2 eggs
½ teaspoon vanilla
½ teaspoon lemon extract
1 pint strawberries

Combine sugar, cornstarch and salt in top part of a double boiler. Stir in milk. Cook over low heat, stirring constantly, until mixture is thick and smooth. Beat eggs slightly. Pour hot mixture slowly over eggs and beat well. Return mixture to top of double boiler and cook over boiling water 5 minutes, stirring constantly. Cool. Stir in flavorings. Pour into tart shell. Wash, hull and halve berries. Arrange on top of custard just before serving. Makes 6 to 8 servings.

Coconut Pumpkin Chiffon Tarts

1 envelope unflavored gelatine
½ cup cold water
2 eggs, separated
1 cup evaporated milk
1¼ cups strained cooked or canned pumpkin
¾ cup firmly packed brown sugar
½ teaspoon salt
½ teaspoon nutmeg
½ teaspoon cinnamon
¼ teaspoon ginger
1 cup toasted shredded coconut
8 baked tart shells
⅓ cup heavy cream, whipped

Soften gelatine in cold water. Put egg yolks in top of double boiler, add evaporated milk and beat until blended. Stir in pumpkin, ½ cup of the brown sugar, salt and spices. Cook over boiling water 10 minutes, stirring constantly. Remove from heat. Add gelatine and stir until dissolved. Chill until slightly thickened. Beat egg whites until stiff, but not dry; add remaining brown sugar gradually and continue beating. Fold pumpkin mixture into egg whites with ¾ cup of the toasted coconut. Fill tart shells and chill until firm. To serve, top with whipped cream and remaining coconut. Makes 8 servings.

Banana Coconut Cream Tarts

¾ cup heavy cream
2 tablespoons sugar
¼ teaspoon vanilla
1 cup moist shredded coconut
6 baked 3½-inch tart shells
3 ripe bananas

Beat cream until stiff. Fold in sugar and vanilla. Sprinkle shredded coconut into tart shells. Peel bananas and slice over coconut. Cover banana slices at once with whipped cream. Garnish tarts with additional coconut and sliced berries if desired. Makes 6 servings.

Streusel Peach Tarts

½ cup sugar
2 tablespoons flour
2 tablespoons butter
¼ teaspoon cinnamon
10 unbaked tart shells
10 well drained canned peach halves

Mix together sugar, flour, butter and cinnamon. Sprinkle half of the crumb mixture in the bottoms of the tart shells. Place a peach half in each tart shell. Sprinkle remaining crumb mixture over peach halves. Bake in a hot oven (425° F) 20 to 30 minutes or until crust is delicately browned. Serve warm. Makes 10 tarts.

Cranberry Tarts

4 cups chopped cranberries
1 teaspoon grated
   orange rind
2 oranges, peeled and
   chopped
2 cups sugar
3 tablespoons quick-cooking
   tapioca

1 tablespoon butter or
   margarine, melted
½ teaspoon salt
1 orange, sectioned
6 mayonnaise pie crust tart
   shells, unbaked

Combine cranberries, orange rind, oranges, sugar, tapioca, margarine and salt. Pour into tart shells. Arrange orange sections on top of filling. Bake in a very hot oven (450° F) 10 minutes; reduce temperature to moderate 350° F and bake 25 to 30 minutes. Makes 6 tarts.

Java Cream Tarts

6 tablespoons flour
⅔ cup sugar
⅛ teaspoon salt
2 cups strong coffee
1 cup evaporated milk

2 eggs, beaten
1 teaspoon vanilla
2 tablespoons butter
8 baked tart shells

Combine flour, sugar and salt in top of a double boiler. Add coffee and milk and mix well. Cook over low heat, stirring constantly, until thick. Pour slowly over beaten eggs, mix well and return to double boiler and cook over boiling water 3 minutes. Add vanilla and butter. Cool. Pour into tart shells and chill thoroughly. Makes 8 tarts.

Fruit Sherbet Tarts

20 graham crackers, finely
   crushed
¼ cup softened butter
   or margarine
¼ cup sugar
1 large banana

¼ cup orange juice
2 tablespoons lime juice
¾ cup sugar
1¼ cups milk
1 egg white

Thoroughly blend together graham cracker crumbs, butter and sugar. Divide mixture into 8 fluted paper cups set in muffin pans. Press crumbs firmly against bottom and sides of paper cups with a spoon or a straight sided glass. Place in freezing compartment of refrigerator. Mash banana with a fork, add orange juice, lime juice and sugar. Stir in milk. Freeze 1 hour. Beat mixture with a rotary beater. Beat egg white until stiff but not dry and fold into sherbet mixture. Spoon sherbet into tart shells. Place in freezing compartment of refrigerator and freeze 3 to 4 hours. Remove fluted paper cups before serving. Makes 8 tarts.

Black and White Tarts

1 cup shredded coconut
1 cup candy-coated rice
cereal or puffed wheat
¼ cup honey
2 tablespoons sugar
¼ teaspoon salt

1 tablespoon butter
1 package vanilla pudding
mix
1 package chocolate pudding
mix

Spread coconut in a shallow baking pan. Bake in a moderate oven (350° F) 5 to 7 minutes, or until delicately browned. Stir or shake often during browning time. Place toasted coconut and cereal in a greased bowl and set aside. Combine honey, sugar and salt in a small saucepan. Bring to a boil over medium heat, stirring to dissolve sugar. Continue boiling until a small amount of syrup forms a firm ball in cold water or to a temperature of 246° F. Add butter. Pour syrup over coconut and cereal and stir lightly to coat. Press mixture on bottom and sides of well greased custard cups or tart tins. Chill. Fill tarts with chocolate and vanilla pudding. Garnish with shaved chocolate and shredded coconut. Makes 6 tarts.

Cheese Apricot Turnovers

3 3-ounce packages
cream cheese
⅓ cup butter
2 cups sifted flour

1 teaspoon salt
½ pound dried apricots,
cooked and puréed
½ cup sugar

Blend together cream cheese and butter. Gradually cut in mixed and sifted dry ingredients; chill. Roll out very thin on a lightly floured board. Cut into 4-inch squares. Combine apricots and sugar. Place 1 tablespoon of the apricot mixture on each square of pastry. Fold squares into triangles and seal edges with a fork. Prick tops with a fork. Place on a cookie sheet. Bake in a moderate oven (375° F) 20 to 25 minutes. Makes 18 to 20 turnovers.

Open-Face Raspberry Tarts

2 tablespoons sugar
1 tablespoon cornstarch
⅛ teaspoon salt
¾ cup fruit juice

1 teaspoon lemon juice
4 to 6 baked tart shells
1 pint fresh raspberries

Blend together in a saucepan sugar, cornstarch and salt. Stir in fruit juice and cook over low heat until thick and clear. Cool. Add lemon juice. Fill tart shells with raspberries. Pour fruit sauce over berries. Chill. Top with whipped cream, if desired. Makes 4 to 6 tarts.

Peach Patisseries

⅓ cup sugar
3 tablespoons flour
½ teaspoon cornstarch
Few grains salt
1 cup milk

2 egg yolks, slightly beaten
¼ teaspoon vanilla
¼ teaspoon almond extract
6 3-inch baked tart shells
6 peach halves

In the top of a double boiler mix together sugar, flour, corn-starch and salt. Stir in milk. Cook over low heat, stirring con-stantly, until thick. Pour slowly into beaten egg yolks, return to double boiler and cook over boiling water 3 minutes. Cool. Add flavorings. Pour mixture into tart shells. Place a peach half on each, cut side up. If desired, garnish with whipped cream. Makes 6 tarts.

The Borden Company

To shape cookie tart shells, invert muffin tins, grease outside of cups. Place rounds over cups, press down and pinch edges of dough at intervals.

Cookie Tart Shells

⅓ cup margarine
½ cup sugar
1 egg
1 tablespoon orange juice

1½ cups sifted flour
1 teaspoon baking powder
¼ teaspoon salt

Cream margarine; add sugar gradually and mix well. Add egg and orange juice; mix well. Sift flour, baking powder and salt together. Add to creamed mixture and blend well. Chill dough. Roll dough on a lightly floured board to ⅛-inch thickness; cut into rounds. Invert muffin tins and grease outside of cups. Place rounds over cups, press down and pinch edges of dough at intervals to fit cups. Prick with a fork. Bake in a moderate oven (375° F) 6 to 8 minutes. Cool 1 minute before removing shells. Fill with berries, pudding or ice cream for serving. Makes 10 or 12 tart shells.

Fig-Nut Turnovers

½ cup sugar
½ cup figs, finely chopped
1 cup finely chopped peeled apple
1 cup almonds, chopped
1 teaspoon grated orange rind

1 cup liquid (juice of 1 orange plus water)
¼ teaspoon cinnamon
¼ teaspoon mace
1 recipe pastry

Combine sugar, figs, apple, almonds, orange rind, liquid, cinnamon and mace in a saucepan. Simmer until thick and apples are soft, about 5 minutes. Cool. Divide dough in halves. Roll out one-half on a lightly floured board to a 15 by 10-inch rectangle. Cut into 5-inch squares. Place a rounded tablespoon of the fig filling on each. Fold squares in half to form rectangles. Seal edges with a fork. Place on a cookie sheet. Prick tops to allow escape of steam. Bake in a hot oven (425° F) 12 to 15 minutes. Makes 12 turnovers.

Banbury Turnovers

1 recipe pastry
½ cup sugar
1 tablespoon flour
1 egg, slightly beaten
1 cup seedless raisins

¼ cup chopped nuts
1 tablespoon lemon juice
2 teaspoons grated lemon rind

Roll pastry out ⅛ inch thick. Cut into twelve 4-inch squares. Combine sugar and flour and stir into beaten egg. Add remaining ingredients and mix well. Place 2 tablespoons of the filling on half of each square and fold over pastry to form a triangle. Seal edges and flute with fingers or a fork. Prick tops with a fork and place on a baking sheet. Bake in a hot oven (425° F) about 15 minutes or until lightly browned. Makes 12 turnovers.

Chocolate Macaroon Tarts

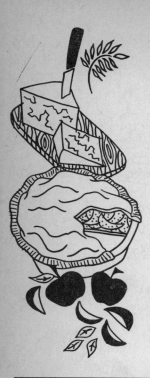

1/4 cup cornstarch
3/4 cup sugar
1/8 teaspoon salt
2 cups milk, scalded
2 eggs, separated
1 tablespoon butter
3 squares unsweetened chocolate, melted

1 teaspoon vanilla
1 1/2 cups macaroon cookie crumbs
2 egg whites, stiffly beaten
8 baked tart shells
1 cup heavy cream, whipped

Mix cornstarch, sugar and salt together in top of a double boiler. Add milk and blend well. Cook over low heat, stirring constantly, until thick. Beat egg yolks. Pour hot mixture slowly over egg yolks and mix well. Return to double boiler. Stir in butter and chocolate. Cook over boiling water 3 minutes. Cool. Add vanilla, macaroon crumbs and egg whites. Fill tart shells. Chill well. Garnish with whipped cream. Makes 8 tarts.

Cranberry Apple Tarts

2 1/2 cups cranberries, coarsely chopped
1 1/2 cups chopped peeled apples
1 1/4 cups sugar

Grated rind of 1 orange
1 tablespoon flour
3 tablespoons water
6 unbaked tart shells

Combine all ingredients except tart shells. Let stand about 10 minutes. Pour into tart shells. Bake in a hot oven (425° F) 25 to 30 minutes. Makes six 2 1/2-inch tarts.

Fruit Pies

Whether you bake a Nectar Mince or Apple Crumb your family will chorus, "Yum! Yum! Yum!"

Nectar Mince Pie

1 recipe spicy pastry
¼ cup butter or margarine
½ cup sugar
½ cup molasses
½ teaspoon salt
2 eggs

1 cup prepared mincemeat
½ cup seedless raisins
½ cup chopped nuts
2 tablespoons grated orange rind

Line a 9-inch pie plate with one-half the pastry. Cream together butter and sugar and blend in molasses and salt. Add eggs one at a time, beating thoroughly after each addition. Add mincemeat, raisins, nuts and orange rind. Pour filling into pastry lined pie plate. Roll out remaining crust and cut into pumpkin shapes. Place on top of filling. Bake in a hot oven (400° F) 30 to 40 minutes. Makes one 9-inch pie.

The Borden Company

Corn Products Company

Metropolitan Apple Pie

1 recipe pastry
1 cup sugar
1⅓ cups pineapple juice
½ teaspoon salt
6 medium-size apples

2 teaspoons cornstarch
½ teaspoon vanilla
2 tablespoons butter or margarine

Line a 9-inch pie plate with half the pastry. Combine sugar, pineapple juice and salt and heat to boiling. Peel, core and quarter apples. Simmer in pineapple juice until tender, moving apples just enough to keep them covered with syrup. Lift the apples out carefully and arrange in pastry shell. Blend cornstarch with a little cold water and add to syrup. Cook over low heat until syrup thickens. Add the vanilla and butter and pour over apples. Roll out remaining pastry and cut in a long strip. Starting at center of pie, twist and coil the strip over the apples to form a curled spiral top crust. Bake in a hot oven (450° F) 10 minutes and then reduce the heat to moderate 375° F and bake about 20 minutes. Makes one 9-inch pie.

National Dairy Council

Apple Crumb Pie

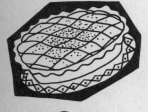

6 tart apples, peeled,
  cored and sliced
2 tablespoons butter, melted
¾ cup sugar
½ teaspoon nutmeg
½ teaspoon cinnamon
⅛ teaspoon salt

1 9-inch unbaked pie shell
½ cup brown sugar,
  firmly packed
¼ cup flour
¼ cup butter or margarine
½ cup chopped nuts

Mix together apples, butter, sugar, nutmeg, cinnamon and salt. Arrange in the pie shell. Combine brown sugar and flour. Cut in the butter and add nuts. Sprinkle evenly over apples. Bake in a moderate oven (375° F) about 50 minutes, or until apples are tender. Serve warm or cold. Makes one 9-inch pie.

Peach Pie

1 recipe pastry
¼ to ½ cup sugar
¼ cup flour or 3 tablespoons
  quick-cooking tapioca
½ teaspoon cinnamon

Dash of nutmeg
6 cups sliced fresh peaches
1 tablespoon lemon juice
Butter or margarine

Line a 9-inch pie plate with half the pastry. Combine sugar
flour, cinnamon, nutmeg and peaches. Place in pie plate. Sprinkl
with lemon juice and dot with butter. Cover with top crust. Bak
in a hot oven (450° F) 10 minutes; reduce heat to moderat
375° F and bake 30 to 40 minutes. Makes one 9-inch pie.

Dutch Peach Pie

6 fresh peaches
1 9-inch unbaked pie shell
1 cup sugar
¼ teaspoon salt

2 tablespoon cornstarch or
  quick-cooking tapioca
1 cup cream
1 teaspoon vanilla

Peel peaches. Remove stones and cut in eighths. Arrange in
pie shell. Mix sugar, salt and cornstarch thoroughly. Add cream
and vanilla and pour over peaches. Bake in a hot oven (450° F)
15 minutes; reduce temperature to 325° F and bake 30 minutes
longer or until peaches are tender. Makes one 9-inch pie.

Apricot Pie

1 recipe pastry
⅔ cup sugar
¼ teaspoon salt
1 tablespoon cornstarch
  or quick-cooking tapioca

3½ cups drained, cooked or
  canned apricots
½ cup apricot juice
2 tablespoons lemon juice
1 tablespoon butter

Line a 9-inch pie plate with half the pastry. Mix sugar, salt
and cornstarch. Add apricots, apricot juice and lemon juice.
Place in pastry lined pie plate and dot top with butter. Cover with
top crust. Bake in a hot oven (425° F) 10 minutes; reduce temperature to 350° F and continue baking about 25 minutes or
until crust is browned. Makes one 9-inch pie.

Cranberry Apple Pie

1 recipe pastry
4 cups peeled, cored and
  sliced apples
¼ cup sugar
2 tablespoons flour

¼ teaspoon salt
1 can whole cranberry sauce
2 teaspoons lemon juice
1 teaspoon grated lemon rind

Line a 9-inch pie plate with half the pastry. Arrange apples in pie plate. Combine remaining ingredients and pour over sliced apples. Cover with a lattice crust. Bake in a hot oven (425° F) 10 minutes. Reduce heat to moderate 350° F and bake 35 minutes longer. Makes one 9-inch pie.

Apple Crunch Pie

1 recipe pastry
5 cups pared, sliced apples
¾ cup sugar
¼ teaspoon cinnamon
¼ teaspoon salt
1 tablespoon flour
1 tablespoon lemon juice

1 tablespoon butter or
  margarine
Topping:
1 tablespoon shortening
1 tablespoon sugar
3 tablespoons flour
¼ teaspoon salt

Line a 9-inch pie plate with one-half the pastry. Combine apples with sugar, cinnamon, salt, flour and lemon juice. Place in pastry lined pie plate. Dot the top with butter. Cover with top crust. Mix topping ingredients of shortening, sugar, flour and salt until crumbly. Sprinkle over top of pie. Bake in a hot oven (425° F) about 10 minutes; reduce temperature to 350° F and continue baking about 25 to 30 minutes or until apples are tender and crust is browned. Makes one 9-inch pie.

Cranberry Pineapple Pie

1 cup sugar
3 tablespoons flour
¼ teaspoon salt
½ cup corn syrup
½ cup pineapple syrup

4 cups washed cranberries
4 slices canned pineapple,
  cut in pieces
1 teaspoon grated lemon rind
1 9-inch unbaked pie shell

Combine sugar, flour, salt, corn syrup and pineapple syrup. Bring to a boil over low heat. Add cranberries and cook gently until skins pop. Remove from heat and add pineapple and lemon rind. Cool slightly without stirring. Pour into pie shell. Bake in a hot oven (425° F) 10 minutes; reduce heat to moderate 350° F and bake 30 minutes longer. Makes one 9-inch pie.

Lattice Top Cherry Pie

1 recipe pastry
2½ to 3 tablespoons quick-cooking tapioca
1 cup sugar
⅛ teaspoon salt

4 cups (two No. 2 cans) drained, pitted red sour cherries, water packed
½ cup cherry juice
1 tablespoon butter or margarine

Line a 9-inch pie pan with half the pastry. Combine tapioca, sugar, salt, cherries and juice. Fill pie shell with cherry mixture and dot with butter. Cover with a lattice crust. Bake in a hot oven (425° F) 45 minutes, or until syrup boils with heavy bubbles that do not burst. Makes one 9-inch pie.

Corn Products Company

Individual Deep-Dish Apple Pie

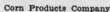

6 to 8 medium apples	1 teaspoon grated lemon rind
1 tablespoon cornstarch or quick-cooking tapioca	1 teaspoon lemon juice
1 teaspoon cinnamon	3 tablespoons butter or margarine, melted
¼ teaspoon salt	1 cup corn syrup
¼ cup sugar	½ recipe pastry

Peel and core apples. Cut in wedges about ¼ inch thick. Arrange in 4 small casseroles. Combine remaining ingredients, except pastry; stir until blended. Pour mixture evenly over apples. Roll pastry and cut in four small circles to fit casseroles. Cut slashes to allow escape of steam. Place over apples and seal edges. Bake in a hot oven (450° F) for ten minutes, reduce temperature to moderate 350° F and bake for 30 minutes or until apples are tender. Makes 4 individual pies.

Prune and Apricot Pie

1 tablespoon flour
6 tablespoons sugar
1 cup prune and apricot juice
2 tablespoons lemon juice
Grated rind of 1 lemon

2 tablespoons butter or margarine
1 cup cooked dried apricots
1 cup cooked dried prunes
1 recipe pastry

Mix flour and sugar thoroughly. Add fruit juices and mix well. Cook over low heat, stirring until thick. Remove from heat and add rind, butter, apricots and prunes. Let cool. Line an 8-inch pie plate with half the pastry. Turn prune mixture into lined pie dish. Cover with lattice top. Bake in a hot oven (450° F) 20 to 25 minutes. Makes one 8-inch pie.

Caramel Apple Pie

3½ cups canned apple slices
1 9-inch unbaked pie shell
¾ cup sugar
¾ cup graham cracker crumbs
¼ cup flour
Dash of salt

½ cup chopped pecans
½ teaspoon cinnamon
⅓ cup butter or margarine, melted
¼ pound caramels
¼ cup hot water

Place apple slices in pie shell. Combine sugar, crumbs, flour, salt, pecans, cinnamon and butter. Sprinkle mixture over apple slices. Bake in a hot oven (450° F) 10 minutes; reduce temperature to moderate 350° F and continue baking 20 minutes. Combine caramels and hot water in top of a double boiler. Cook over hot water, stirring frequently, until caramels are melted and sauce smooth. Pour mixture over top of crumbs on apple pie. Return to oven and continue baking for 10 minutes. Makes one 9-inch pie.

French Apple Pie

4 to 5 large apples
¾ cup sugar
½ teaspoon cinnamon
½ teaspoon salt

2 tablespoons flour
1 9-inch unbaked pie shell
½ cup cream

Pare, core and slice apples. Combine sugar, cinnamon, salt and flour. Sprinkle half the mixture in the bottom of pie shell. Place apple slices on dry ingredients. Sprinkle remaining dry mixture on top of apples. Pour cream over apples. Bake in a hot oven (400° F) 15 minutes; reduce temperature to 350° F and continue baking 45 to 60 minutes until apples are tender. Makes one 9-inch pie.

Strawberry Glaze Pie

1 quart ripe strawberries
¾ cup water
1 cup sugar
3 tablespoons cornstarch
1 teaspoon lemon juice

2 3-ounce packages cream
  cheese
4 tablespoons cream
1 9-inch baked pie shell

Wash and hull strawberries; drain well. Combine 1 cup of the berries with water and simmer 5 minutes. Reserve remaining berries. Mix sugar and cornstarch together. Stir in cooked berries and cook, stirring constantly, until syrup is clear and thick. Stir in lemon juice and cool slightly. Mix together cheese and cream until light and fluffy. Spread over bottom of baked pie shell. Cover with remaining whole berries. Pour thickened syrup over top of berries. Chill well before serving. Makes one 9-inch pie.

Deep Dish Rhubarb Pie

2 pounds rhubarb, cut in ½
  inch pieces
1¼ cups sugar
¼ cup flour or 3 tablespoons
  quick cooking tapioca
⅛ teaspoon nutmeg

2 tablespoons shredded
  orange rind
2 tablespoons butter or
  margarine
½ recipe pastry

Combine rhubarb with sugar, flour, nutmeg and orange rind and mix lightly. Place in 8-inch square pan and dot with butter. Top with pastry. Bake in a hot oven (425° F) 30 minutes. Makes 4 to 6 servings.

Paradise Pie

6 large apples
¾ cup sugar
1 tablespoon red cinnamon
  candies
4 tablespoons orange juice
1 tablespoon lemon juice

1 tablespoon grated lemon
  rind
1 9-inch baked pie shell
1 cup whipped cream
¼ cup chopped nuts

Wash, pare and core apples. Cut each apple in eight sections. Arrange in a large saucepan, add the sugar, cinnamon candies and enough water to just cover apples. Simmer until tender, turning often. Remove apples and place in a dish. To the remaining syrup in the saucepan add orange juice, lemon juice and lemon rind. Simmer until syrup is thick. Pour over apples and let stand until cool. Arrange apple sections in the baked pie shell. Chill thoroughly. Garnish with whipped cream and nuts before serving. Makes one 9-inch pie.

French Peach Pie

1 ½ cups sifted flour
½ teaspoon salt
½ cup shortening
2 to 3 tablespoons cold
   water
4 cups sliced fresh peaches

½ cup granulated sugar
¾ cup brown sugar, firmly
   packed, divided
1 tablespoon lemon juice
3 tablespoons cornstarch

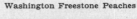

Sift together flour and salt. Cut in shortening with a
pastry blender or two knives. Measure ½ cup of the flour-
shortening mixture and set aside. Sprinkle remaining flour
mixture with cold water, tossing lightly with a fork until
dough forms a ball. Roll out and fit into a 9-inch pie plate.
Flute edges. Combine peaches, sugar, ½ cup of brown sugar,
lemon juice and cornstarch. Toss lightly. Place in pie shell.
Combine reserve flour mixture and remaining ¼ cup brown
sugar. Sprinkle over top of peach filling. Bake in a hot oven
(425°F.) 45 to 50 minutes. Makes 1 pie.

Washington Freestone Peaches

Crunchy Pear Pie

¼ cup sugar
2 tablespoons cornstarch
⅛ teaspoon salt
½ teaspoon ginger, divided
1½ cups juice drained from pears
1 teaspoon grated lemon rind

1 tablespoon lemon juice
2 cups pear halves, drained
1 unbaked 9-inch pie shell
1 cup sifted flour
½ cup brown sugar, firmly packed
½ cup butter or margarine
½ cup chopped nuts

Combine sugar, corn starch, salt and ¼ teaspoon ginger in a saucepan. Blend in pear juice. Cook over medium heat, stirring constantly, until mixture thickens and comes to a boil. Remove from heat. Add lemon rind and lemon juice. Cut pear halves in half lengthwise, arrange in pastry shell. Pour thickened syrup over top of pears. Blend together flour, brown sugar, butter and remaining sugar with a pastry blender until mixture looks like coarse crumbs. Stir in nuts. Sprinkle over top of pears. Bake in a hot oven (425°F.) 20 to 25 minutes. Makes one 9-inch pie.

Best Foods, Inc.

Rhubarb Pie

1 recipe pastry
4 cups cut rhubarb
1 cup sugar
⅓ cup light brown sugar
¼ teaspoon salt

6 tablespoons flour or
  5 tablespoons quick cooking tapioca
¼ teaspoon cinnamon
2 tablespoons butter or
  margarine

Line a 9-inch pie plate with half the pastry. Combine rhubarb, sugars, salt, flour and cinnamon and pour into pie shell. Dot top with butter. Cover with a lattice top. Bake in a hot oven (400° F) 45 minutes. Makes one 9-inch pie.

Raspberry Glaze Pie with Gingersnap Crust

⅓ cup melted margarine
1¼ cups gingersnap crumbs
2 tablespoons confectioners'
  sugar
½ teaspoon cinnamon
1 pint raspberries
⅓ cup sugar
2 teaspoons unflavored
  gelatine

1½ tablespoons cold water
2 tablespoons melted
  margarine
½ teaspoon lemon juice
1 package prepared vanilla
  pudding
½ teaspoon almond extract
1 cup cream, whipped

Add margarine to gingersnap crumbs; stir in confectioners' sugar and cinnamon and blend well. Spread in a 9-inch pie plate. Pat mixture firmly onto bottom and sides. Bake in a hot oven (400° F) 10 minutes. Cool. Combine raspberries and sugar in a saucepan; heat gently. Strain off juice and set raspberries aside. Soften gelatine in water; dissolve over hot water. Stir into berry juice; add margarine and lemon juice. Cool until slightly thickened. Meanwhile, prepare pudding according to directions on package; add almond extract. Cool and pour into gingersnap shell. Spread raspberries over pudding and cover with gelatine mixture. Chill until set. Before serving, spread with whipped cream and garnish with additional raspberries. Makes one 9-inch pie.

Apricot Crumb Pie

1 9-inch unbaked pie shell
4 cups sliced fresh apricots
½ cup sugar
¼ teaspoon nutmeg

¾ cup flour
¼ cup firmly packed brown
  sugar
⅓ cup butter

Fill pie shell with apricots mixed with sugar and nutmeg. Mix flour and brown sugar together. Cut in butter until mixture is crumbly. Sprinkle over top of apricots. Bake in a hot oven (400° F) 45 minutes. Makes one 9-inch pie.

Melody Pie

1 cup chopped, cooked, pitted prunes
3½ cups chopped, peeled, cored apples
1 tablespoon grated orange rind
¼ cup orange juice

2 tablespoons flour
½ teaspoon salt
½ cup sugar
¼ cup prune juice
¼ cup molasses
1 9-inch unbaked pie shell
1 cup whipped cream

Mix prunes, apples, orange rind and juice. Mix together dry ingredients, prune juice and molasses. Add to prune mixture and pour into pastry shell. Bake in a hot oven (450° F) 10 minutes; reduce temperature to 375° F and continue baking 50 minutes. Cool before serving. Garnish with whipped cream. Makes one 9-inch pie.

Mock Mince Pie

½ lemon
1½ cups raisins
2 apples, unpeeled, cored and chopped
½ cup suet
¼ cup sugar
½ cup molasses

½ teaspoon salt
½ teaspoon cinnamon
¼ teaspoon allspice
¼ teaspoon ground cloves
⅓ cup boiling water
1 beef bouillon cube
1 recipe pastry

Put lemon and raisins through food chopper. Add remaining ingredients, except pastry. Heat to boiling and simmer, stirring occasionally, about 30 minutes. Cool slightly. Line a 9-inch pie plate with about two-thirds of the pastry. Pour filling into pie plate. Cover with lattice top. Bake in a hot oven (450° F) 10 minutes; reduce temperature to 350° F and continue baking 30 to 40 minutes. Makes one 9-inch pie.

Winter Fruit Pie

1 recipe pastry
2 cups raw cranberries
2 cups peeled, chopped apples
½ cup water
½ cup sugar

2 tablespoons flour
½ cup corn syrup
Dash of salt
½ teaspoon grated orange rind

Line a 9-inch pie plate with half the pastry. Cook cranberries and apples in water until cranberries pop, about 5 minutes. Add sugar and blend. Cover and allow to cool. Add flour, corn syrup, salt and orange rind. Mix well and pour into pastry lined pie plate. Cover with lattice top. Bake in a hot oven (425° F) 35 to 45 minutes. Makes one 9-inch pie.

Apple-Peach Pie

1 recipe pastry
2 cups sliced apples
1 cup sugar
¼ cup flour or
  3 tablespoons tapioca

2 teaspoons cinnamon
⅛ teaspoon cloves
¼ teaspoon salt
2 cups sliced peaches

Line a 9-inch pie plate with half the pastry. Arrange apples in bottom of pie plate. Combine sugar, flour, cinnamon, cloves and salt. Sprinkle apples with half of this mixture. Top with sliced peaches and sprinkle with remaining dry ingredients. Cover with top crust. Bake in a hot oven (425° F) 10 minutes: reduce heat to 375° F and continue baking 20 to 30 minutes or until apples are done. Makes one 9-inch pie.

Fresh Apricot Pie

1 recipe pastry
⅔ cup sugar
1 cup pineapple juice
1½ dozen fresh apricots,
  pitted and halved

2 teaspoons cornstarch
½ teaspoon salt
2 tablespoons margarine
½ teaspoon vanilla

Line a 9-inch pie plate with half the pastry. Combine sugar and pineapple juice and boil 1 minute. Simmer apricots, a few at a time, until just tender. Lift apricots carefully from juice and arrange in pie shell. Mix cornstarch with a little cold water; add to juice and cook until thickened. Add salt, margarine and vanilla and pour over apricots. Cover with lattice top. Bake in a hot oven (450° F) 10 minutes; reduce heat to 350° F and bake about 20 minutes. Makes one 9-inch pie.

Corn Products Company

Deep Dish Prune and Apricot Pies

1½ cups cooked prunes,
    drained
1½ cups cooked apricots,
    drained
1 tablespoon cornstarch
    or quick-cooking tapioca
¼ teaspoon salt

2 tablespoons lemon juice
1 tablespoon grated lemon
    rind
1½ tablespoons melted
    butter or margarine
1 cup corn syrup
1 recipe pastry

Pit and halve prunes. Mix with apricots and place in 6 individual deep pie dishes. Combine remaining ingredients except pastry; stir until blended. Pour mixture equally over fruit. Roll pastry ⅛ inch thick and cut in narrow strips. Arrange in a lattice pattern across top of pies. Make a rim with one long strip. Bake in a hot oven (450° F) 10 minutes; reduce heat to moderate 350° F and bake 35 minutes longer or until crust is brown. Makes 6 deep dish pies.

Cherry Almond Pie

1 recipe pastry
4 cups fresh sour cherries
¾ cup sugar
2 tablespoons flour or 1½ tablespoons quick-cooking tapioca

⅛ teaspoon salt
2 tablespoons butter or margarine
¼ cup blanched slivered almonds

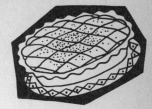

Line a 9-inch pie plate with half the pastry. Wash, pit and drain cherries. Combine with sugar, flour and salt. Pour into lined pie plate. Dot top with butter. Cover with a lattice top. Sprinkle almonds over top of pie. Bake in a hot oven (400° F) about 45 minutes. Makes one 9-inch pie.

Eggnog Pear Pie

1 can (1 pound) pear halves
1 envelope unflavored gelatine
1½ cups eggnog

⅓ cup heavy cream
3 tablespoons brandy
8-inch graham cracker crumb shell
Nutmeg

Drain pear halves, reserving syrup. Soften gelatine in 1/3 cup pear syrup. Heat over hot water until dissolved. Stir in eggnog and chill until syrupy. Whip cream. Whip eggnog-gelatine mixture. Fold whipped cream and brandy into gelatine mixture. Slice three pear halves and place in bottom of pie shell. Pour eggnog mixture over sliced pears. Chill until firm. Slice remaining pear halves. Dip edges in nutmeg and use to garnish top of pie. Makes 6 servings.

Bartlett Pears

Blueberry Pie

3 tablespoons quick-cooking
  tapioca
¾ to 1 cup sugar*
¼ teaspoon salt
⅛ teaspoon cinnamon
4 cups wild or cultivated
  fresh blueberries

1 to 2 tablespoons lemon
  juice
Pastry for two-crust 9-inch
  pie
1 tablespoon butter

Combine tapioca, sugar, salt, cinnamon, blueberries and lemon juice. Roll half the pastry ⅛ inch thick. Line a 9-inch pie pan and trim pastry at edge of rim. Roll remaining pastry ⅛ inch thick and cut several 2-inch slits or a fancy design near center. Fill pie shell with blueberry mixture. Dot with butter. Moisten edge of bottom crust. To adjust top crust, fold pastry in half or roll loosely on rolling pin; center on filling. Open slits with a knife. (Well-opened slits are important to permit escape of steam during baking.) Trim top crust, allowing it to extend ½ inch over rim. To seal, press top and bottom crusts together on rim. Then fold edge of top crust under bottom crust and flute. Bake in hot oven (425° F) 55 minutes, or until syrup boils with heavy bubbles that do not burst. Makes one 9-inch pie.

*If desired, ½ cup granulated sugar and ½ cup firmly packed brown sugar may be used.

Raspberry Pie

1 pint red raspberries,
divided
¾ cup water
½ cup sugar
1 tablespoon cornstarch
1½ teaspoons unflavored
gelatine

2 tablespoons cold water
1 tablespoon lemon juice
1 9-inch cereal flake pie
shell
1 cup whipped cream

Cook one cup of raspberries with water for 5 minutes. Strain.
Mix sugar and cornstarch; add hot raspberry juice and cook,
stirring constantly, until thickened and clear. Soften gelatine
in cold water. Dissolve in hot raspberry mixture. Cool until
the consistency of unbeaten egg whites. Fold in remaining
raspberries and lemon juice. Turn into pie shell. Chill in
refrigerator until pie is firm enough to cut. Garnish with
whipped cream before serving. Makes one 9-inch pie.

Strawberry Pie

1 quart strawberries
½ cup sugar
1 tablespoon cornstarch

½ cup water
1 9-inch baked pie shell
1 cup heavy cream, whipped

Wash and hull berries. Cut all large and perfect berries into
2 or 3 slices. Take remaining berries and mash. Combine sugar
and cornstarch in a saucepan. Add water and crushed berries.
Cook over low heat until clear and slightly thickened. Cool. Stir
in sliced berries. Spread bottom of pie shell with half the
whipped cream. Add half of berry mixture. Repeat layers.
Chill in refrigerator before serving. Makes one 9-inch pie.

Prune Pie

2 cups cooked prunes
1 orange
½ cup brown sugar, firmly
packed
¼ teaspoon salt
2 tablespoons cornstarch
1 cup liquid from prunes

2 tablespoons butter or
margarine
1 8-inch baked pie shell
2 egg whites
¼ cup sugar
Few drops lemon flavoring

Pit prunes and cut in half. Peel orange, removing white inner
part completely, and dice orange. Combine sugar, salt and cornstarch; add prune liquid and bring to a boil, stirring constantly
until thickened. Add prunes, orange and butter and continue
cooking for 10 minutes, stirring occasionally. Pour into a baked
pie shell. Beat egg whites until stiff but not dry. Add sugar
and flavoring gradually, beating until mixture stands in peaks.
Pile over pie filling. Bake in a hot oven (425° F) 5 to 10 minutes
or until lightly browned. Makes one 8-inch pie.

Blueberry Cheese Pie

1⅔ cups finely rolled
  graham cracker crumbs
¼ cup soft butter or
  margarine
¼ cup brown sugar, firmly
  packed
½ teaspoon cinnamon
1 envelope unflavored
  gelatine
½ cup sugar

¼ teaspoon salt
3 egg yolks
1 cup milk
1 package (8-ounces)
  cream cheese, softened
1 teaspoon vanilla
1 cup heavy cream
½ cup confectioner's sugar
½ cup dairy sour cream
1 teaspoon vanilla
1 cup fresh blueberries

Combine graham cracker crumbs, butter, brown sugar and cinnamon. Pour into a 9-inch pie plate. Press crumbs firmly against bottom and sides of pie plate. Bake in a moderate oven (375°F.) 8 minutes. Cool. Combine gelatine, sugar and salt in top of a double boiler. Beat yolks. Beat in milk. Stir into dry ingredients in top of double boiler. Cook over boiling water, until mixture begins to thicken, about 15 minutes. Slowly add cream cheese and vanilla. Stir until well blended. Cool. Pour into chilled shell. Chill until firm. Whip cream and confectioners' sugar together until it stands in stiff peaks. Continue beating while gradually adding sour cream and vanilla. Fold in blueberries. Spread over cheese filling. Chill thoroughly. Makes one 9-inch pie.

National Biscuit Company

Corn Products Company

Apple Raisin Crumb Pie

6 apples	¼ teaspoon salt
¾ cup raisins	1 cup sugar, divided
1 cup water	1 unbaked 9-inch pie shell
1 tablespoon flour	½ cup margarine, melted
1 teaspoon cinnamon	1 cup quick oats
½ teaspoon nutmeg	½ cup flour

Peel, core and slice apples. Add raisins and water and stew about 10 minutes. Mix flour, spices and 2 tablespoons of the sugar. Add to apples, stir until smooth, and bring to boil. Turn into pie shell. Combine remaining ingredients and sprinkle over top of apples. Bake in a hot oven (450° F) 10 minutes. Reduce heat to moderate 350° F and bake 40 to 45 minutes or until crumbs are brown and crisp. Makes one 9-inch pie.

Processed Apples Institute, Inc.

Cheese-Apple Pie

2½ cups sliced apples
1 cup brown sugar, divided
2 tablespoons flour
1 tablespoon cinnamon
½ teaspoon nutmeg

1 tablespoon lemon juice
⅔ cup flour
⅓ cup butter
⅔ cup grated American cheese

Combine apples, ½ cup sugar, 2 tablespoons flour, cinnamon, nutmeg and lemon juice. Place in deep dish pie pan. Mix remaining ½ cup sugar and 2/3 cup flour; cut in butter with 2 knives or pastry blender. Add cheese, toss lightly; sprinkle mixture over apples. Bake in hot oven (400°F.) for 45-50 minutes. Serve with wedges of cheese on top.

Strawberry Bavarian Pie

1 cup brown sugar
2 .cups rolled oats (quick or old fashioned, uncooked)
⅔ cup butter, melted
2 envelopes unflavored gelatine
½ cup cold water
2 eggs, separated

¼ cup water
¼ cup sugar
Few drops red food coloring
1 tablespoon lemon juice
2 cups crushed fresh strawberries
⅔ cup evaporated milk, chilled
Few Whole Strawberries

Combine brown sugar and oats. Add melted butter. Mix well. Reserve ½ cup of mixture for topping. Press remaining oats mixture onto the bottom and sides of a deep pie plate (9½ x 2 inches). Chill until firm in freezer or refrigerator.

Soften gelatine in ½ cup cold water. Beat together egg yolks, ¼ cup water and sugar. Add a few drops of red food coloring, if desired. Add softened gelatine. Place over low heat (may use double boiler). Stir frequently. Cook until gelatine is dissolved and mixture begins to thicken slightly. Remove from heat; add lemon juice. Cool until thickened; fold in strawberries.

Beat egg whites until stiff. Beat well-chilled evaporated milk until stiff. Fold strawberry mixture into egg whites, then into whipped milk. Pour into crumb-lined pie plate. Sprinkle edge with the ½ cup remaining crumbs. Chill until firm. Garnish with whole strawberries.

The Quaker Oats Company

California Prune Advisory Board

Coffee Coconut Prune Pie

1 cup hot strong coffee
1 can (3½ ounces) flaked coconut
3 tablespoons soft butter
½ pound plumped, pitted chopped prunes, reserve a few whole prunes for garnish
⅓ cup prune juice
2 tablespoons grated orange rind
3 eggs

½ cup brown sugar, firmly packed
¼ cup granulated sugar
1 envelope unflavored gelatine
½ teaspoon salt
1 package (3-ounces) cream cheese, softened
1 cup dairy sour cream
Whipped cream
Maraschino cherries

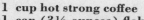

Combine coffee and coconut. Let stand 30 minutes. Drain coconut and spread between pieces of paper toweling and pat dry. Spread softened butter on the bottom and sides of a 9-inch pie plate. Turn coconut into pie plate and pat out to cover bottom and sides of plate. Bake in a moderate oven (350°F.) 10 minutes. Cool. In a saucepan combine chopped prunes, prune juice and orange rind. Bring to a boil and remove from heat. Beat together eggs, brown sugar, granulated sugar, gelatine and salt. Mix in cheese and sour cream and beat until smooth. Stir into prune mixture and cook over moderate heat, stirring constantly, until mixture is smooth and thickened. Cool slightly. Pour mixture into prepared pie shell and chill until firm. Garnish with reserved whole prunes, whipped cream and cherries. Makes one 9-inch pie.

Marmalade Mince Pie

1 recipe pastry
2 cups mincemeat
½ cup orange marmalade
2 tablespoons flour
1 tablespoon lemon juice

Line a 9-inch pie plate with half the pastry. Combine mincemeat, marmalade, flour and lemon juice. Turn into pie plate. Cover with top crust. Bake in a hot oven (425° F) 35 to 40 minutes. Makes one 9-inch pie.

Tangy Apricot Pie

1 pastry recipe
4 cups sliced fresh apricots
¼ cup orange juice
2 teaspoons grated orange rind
½ teaspoon nutmeg
1¼ cups sugar
2½ teaspoons quick-cooking tapioca

Line a 9-inch pie plate with half the pastry. Combine remaining ingredients and pour into pie shell. Cover with top crust. Bake in a hot oven (425°F.) 40 minutes. Makes one 9-inch pie.

Washington Apricots

United Fresh Fruit and Vegetable Association

Cherry Cheese Pie

1 No. 2 can sour red cherries
1 envelope unflavored
  gelatine
½ cup sugar
1 teaspoon grated lemon rind

1 3-ounce package cream
  cheese
1 tablespoon milk
1 9-inch baked pie shell

Drain cherries. To the juice add enough water to make 1½ cups of liquid. Place in a saucepan with the gelatine, sugar and lemon rind. Bring almost to a boil over very low heat. Cool until the consistency of unbeaten egg white. Mix cream cheese and milk together until smooth. Spread on the bottom of the pie shell. Spread cherries over cheese. Pour syrup over cherries. Chill in the refrigerator until firm. Makes one 9-inch pie.

Banana-Apple Pie

2 cups sliced bananas
1 9-inch baked pie shell
1 tablespoon lemon juice

2 cups sweetened applesauce
1 cup heavy cream, whipped
and sweetened

Place sliced bananas on bottom of baked pie shell. Sprinkle with lemon juice. Pour applesauce over bananas and top with whipped cream. Chill well. Makes one 9-inch pie.

Sweet Red Cherry Pie

1 recipe pastry
1½ pounds large sweet
cherries
⅔ cup sugar
1 tablespoon lemon juice

1 teaspoon grated lemon rind
⅛ teaspoon allspice
¼ teaspoon salt
3 tablespoons flour or 2½
tablespoons quick-cooking
tapioca

Line a 9-inch pie plate with half the pastry. Remove stones from cherries with a sharp knife. Toss cherries with remaining ingredients. Pour into pie plate. Cover with lattice top. Bake in a hot oven (425° F) 30 minutes; reduce temperature to moderate 350° F and continue baking until fruit is tender, about 15 minutes. Makes one 9-inch pie.

Raisin Nut Pie

1 recipe pastry
¾ cup water
2 cups raisins
1 tablespoon vinegar
1 tablespoon butter or
margarine

½ cup chopped nuts
⅔ cup sugar
1 tablespoon flour
¼ teaspoon salt

Line an 8-inch pie plate with one-half the pastry. Combine water and raisins and simmer until about ¼ of the liquid remains. Add vinegar, butter and nuts. Cool slightly. Combine sugar, flour and salt. Stir into raisin nut mixture. Pour into pastry lined pie plate. Cover with top crust. Bake in a very hot oven (450° F) 10 minutes; reduce heat to moderate F and bake for 25 minutes. Serve slightly warm. Makes 8-inch pie.

Citrus Prune Pie

3 cups cooked, pitted prunes
1 cup prune juice
4 tablespoons lemon juice
½ cup corn syrup
2 tablespoons cornstarch
⅛ teaspoon salt
1 tablespoon water
1 8-inch baked pie shell
Orange sections

Combine prunes, juices and corn syrup in saucepan. Stir in cornstarch, salt and water. Cook over low heat until thickened, about 15 minutes, stirring occasionally. Cool. Pour into baked pie shell and garnish with orange sections. Makes one 8-inch pie.

Apple Sunday Pie

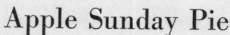

1 cup chocolate wafer crumbs
⅔ cup finely chopped pecans
¼ cup softened (or melted) butter or margarine
1 quart vanilla ice cream
1½ cups shredded fresh, peeled apple
½ cup pecan halves
Unpeeled apple slices for garnish
½ pint heavy cream, whipped

Mix wafer crumbs, pecans and butter or margarine together until crumbly. Press onto bottom and sides of a 9-inch pie plate. Bake in moderate oven (375°F.) about 7 minutes. Chill thoroughly until well set. Soften ice cream and combine with shredded apple. Spread apple-ice cream mixture into pie shell. Sprinkle with pecans. Place in freezer or keep thoroughly chilled until ready to serve; then garnish with thin, unpeeled apple slices. Before serving, top the pie with whipped cream and then garnish with the apple slices if you wish.

Blueberry Meringue Pie

1½ cups fresh cultivated
  blueberries
3 cups cornflakes (about
  1½ cups crumbs)
2 tablespoons sugar
4 tablespoons butter

4 egg whites
¾ cup sugar
½ teaspoon almond extract
¼ teaspoon salt
½ teaspoon cream of
  tartar

Rinse fresh cultivated blueberries and spread between layers of absorbent towels to dry thoroughly. Crush cornflakes to make 1½ cups of crumbs. Mix crumbs with 2 tablespoons sugar. Let butter soften to room temperature and mix cornflake crumbs and butter together thoroughly. Use crumb mixture to line a 9-inch pie plate, pressing crumbs with back of spoon to get an even layer on bottom and sides of pie plate. Bake shell in moderate oven (375°F.) for 10 minutes. Let cool. Beat egg whites until stiff. Gradually add sugar in very small amounts, beating continuously after each addition. Alternately add almond extract, salt and cream of tartar, beating until thick and glossy. Carefully fold in dried blueberries, being careful not to break the berries. Pile blueberry meringue into baked crumb crust. With back of wet tablespoon, make swirl designs in meringue. Bake at 300°F. for about 15 minutes or just until top browns slightly. Let cool before cutting. Makes 8 servings.

Chiffon Pies

From Chocolate Imperial to Strawberry Fluff, you can make 'em and bake 'em 'till you've had enough!

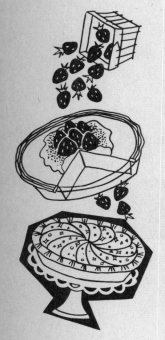

Coffee Rum Chiffon Pie

1 9-inch chocolate crumb crust
1 envelope unflavored gelatine
3 tablespoons rum
⅓ cup sugar
¼ teaspoon salt
⅛ teaspoon cinnamon
3 egg yolks, beaten
1 cup strong cold coffee
3 egg whites
½ teaspoon vanilla
⅓ cup sugar

In the top of a double boiler away from the heat, mix the gelatine and rum. Let stand 5 minutes. Add the first ⅓ cup sugar, salt, cinnamon and egg yolks. Gradually add the coffee, a little at a time, beating briskly after each addition. When thoroughly blended, place over hot water and cook, stirring constantly, until the mixture makes a readily visible film on the back of a silver spoon. Remove from heat and chill thoroughly. Beat egg whites until stiff. Add vanilla and the second ⅓ cup sugar, gradually, beating after each addition. Fold egg whites into the coffee mixture. Pour into the crumb shell and chill until firm. Garnish with whipped cream and shaved chocolate.

Knox Gelatine

Chocolate Imperial Pie

1 envelope unflavored gelatine
¼ cup cold water
3 squares unsweetened chocolate
¼ teaspoon salt

2 egg whites
¼ cup sugar
¾ cup dark corn syrup
½ teaspoon vanilla
1 9-inch baked pie shell

Soften gelatine in cold water. Dissolve over boiling water. Melt chocolate over hot water. Add salt to egg whites and beat until mixture forms soft peaks. Gradually add sugar, beating until smooth and glossy. Continue beating and add corn syrup gradually. Fold in vanilla, cooled gelatine and cooled chocolate. Turn into pie shell. Chill for 3 hours or until firm. If desired, garnish with whipped cream and grated chocolate. Makes one 9-inch pie.

Strawberry Chiffon Pie

1 envelope unflavored gelatine
2 tablespoons cold water
2 egg yolks
¾ cup white corn syrup
1 cup crushed strawberries

1 tablespoon lemon juice
2 egg whites
⅛ teaspoon salt
2 tablespoons sugar
¾ cup heavy cream, whipped
1 9-inch baked pie shell

Soften gelatine in cold water. Beat egg yolks slightly in top of a double boiler. Add corn syrup. Cook over boiling water about 5 minutes, stirring constantly. Add gelatine and stir until dissolved. Cool slightly. Combine strawberries and lemon juice and add to gelatine mixture. Chill until slightly thickened. Beat egg whites and salt until stiff but not dry; gradually beat in sugar. Fold in strawberry mixture; then fold in whipped cream. Pile into baked pie shell. Chill thoroughly. Makes one 9-inch pie.

Peppermint Chiffon Pie

1 envelope unflavored gelatine
¼ cup water
3 egg whites
½ cup sugar
¼ teaspoon peppermint flavoring

¼ cup chopped almonds
½ cup crushed peppermint stick candy
1 cup heavy cream, whipped
1 9-inch chocolate cookie crust

Soften gelatine in cold water; then dissolve over hot water. Beat egg whites until stiff. Gradually beat in sugar. Add gelatine, flavoring, almonds and candy. Fold in whipped cream. Pour into cookie crust and chill until firm. Makes one 9-inch pie.

Sherry Chiffon Pie

1 envelope unflavored gelatine
¼ cup cold water
½ cup boiling water
½ cup sugar

½ cup sherry
½ cup evaporated milk, chilled icy cold
2 tablespoons lemon juice
1 9-inch baked crumb crust

Soften gelatine in cold water. Add boiling water and stir until completely dissolved. Stir in sugar and sherry. Cool until the consistency of unbeaten egg whites. Whip milk until stiff. Fold in lemon juice and gelatine mixture. Pour into crust and chill until firm. Makes one 9-inch pie.

Florida Chiffon Pie

1 envelope unflavored gelatine
1¼ cups orange juice
⅔ cup sugar
1 tablespoon flour
¼ teaspoon salt

1 tablespoon grated orange rind
2 tablespoons lime juice
1 cup heavy cream, whipped
1 9-inch chocolate cookie crumb crust or
9 baked tart shells

Combine gelatine, orange juice, sugar, flour and salt. Place over medium heat; stir constantly until gelatine is dissolved and mixture is slightly thickened. Remove from heat; add orange rind, and lime juice. Chill until mixture is slightly thicker than the consistency of unbeaten egg white. Fold into whipped cream. Turn into pie crust or tart shells and chill until firm. If desired, garnish with whipped cream, orange sections and shaved chocolate. Makes one 9-inch pie.

Lime Chiffon Pie

1 package lime-flavored gelatin
⅛ teaspoon salt
2 tablespoons sugar
1 cup hot water
½ cup cold water

2 to 3 tablespoons lime juice
1½ teaspoons grated lime rind
⅓ cup cream, whipped
1 9-inch baked quick coconut pie crust, cooled

Dissolve gelatin, salt and sugar in *hot* water. Add cold water, lime juice and grated lime rind. Chill until slightly thickened. Then place in bowl of ice and water and whip with rotary beater until fluffy and thick like whipped cream. Fold in whipped cream. Turn into pie shell and chill until firm. Garnish with additional whipped cream, if desired. Makes one 9-inch pie.

Chocolate Bavarian Pie

Best Foods, Inc.

1 envelope unflavored
    gelatine
¼ cup cold water
1 cup fortified chocolate
    flavored syrup

1 pint heavy cream
½ teaspoon vanilla
1 baked 9-inch pastry shell

Soften gelatine in cold water. Heat chocolate syrup in a medium saucepan to a full boil. Remove from heat. Add softened gelatine and stir until gelatine is completely dissolved. Chill until mixture is thick and syrupy, stirring once or twice while chilling. Beat cream until stiff and fold into slightly thickened chocolate-gelatine mixture. Fold in vanilla. Pile into baked pastry shell and chill until firm.

Note: Rum or rum flavoring may be substituted for the vanilla. Use 1 teaspoon rum extract or 1 to 2 tablespoons rum.

Fresh Fruit Chiffon Pie

¼ cup sugar
1 tablespoon lemon juice
1 pint prepared fresh strawberries, sliced
1 envelope unflavored gelatine
¼ cup cold water

¼ teaspoon salt
Water to make ½ cup liquid
3 egg whites
½ cup light corn syrup
1 (9-inch) baked pastry shell

Sprinkle 2 tablespoons of the sugar and the lemon juice over strawberries; let stand 30 minutes. Soften gelatine in ¼ cup cold water. Mix together the remaining sugar and salt in a saucepan. Drain juice from strawberries and add water to make ½ cup liquid; add to sugar and stir over low heat, add softened gelatine and stir until dissolved. Add strawberries. Chill until the consistency of unbeaten egg white.

Caution: Do not let gelatine mixture become too stiff. Beat egg whites until stiff, not dry. Gradually beat in the corn syrup. Fold in chilled gelatine mixture. Chill until thick enough to pile up. Pile lightly into baked pastry shell and swirl gently with a spatula.

Best Foods, Inc.

Lemon Chiffon Pie

1 envelope unflavored gelatine
¼ cup cold water
1 cup sugar, divided
½ cup lemon juice
½ teaspoon salt
4 egg yolks, beaten
1 teaspoon grated lemon rind
4 egg whites
1 8-inch baked pie shell
½ cup heavy cream, whipped

Soften gelatine in cold water. Add ½ cup of the sugar, lemon juice and salt to beaten egg yolks in top of double boiler; cook over boiling water until thick. Add lemon rind and softened gelatine. Stir until gelatine is dissolved. Cool. Beat egg whites until stiff. Gradually beat in sugar until mixture is smooth and glossy. Fold egg whites into gelatine mixture. Pour into baked pie shell. Chill until firm. Just before serving garnish with whipped cream. Makes one 8-inch pie.

Coconut Pie

1 envelope unflavored gelatine
½ cup sugar
¼ teaspoon salt
3 eggs, separated
1¼ cups milk
½ teaspoon almond flavoring
¾ cup flaked coconut, divided
1 9-inch graham cracker crust
¼ cup chopped toasted almonds

Combine gelatine, sugar and salt in top of a double boiler. Stir in beaten egg yolks and milk. Cook over hot water, stirring constantly, until mixture coats a silver spoon. Chill until mixture is consistency of unbeaten egg whites. Add flavoring and ½ cup of the coconut. Beat egg whites until stiff and fold into gelatine mixture. Pour gelatine mixture into pie crust. Chill until firm. Combine remaining coconut and almonds and sprinkle over pie just before serving. Makes one 9-inch pie.

Toffee Chiffon Pie

1 envelope unflavored gelatine
⅔ cup sugar, divided
⅛ teaspoon salt
2 eggs, separated
⅓ cup molasses
1 cup milk
½ cup heavy cream, whipped
1 9-inch baked pie shell

Combine gelatine, ⅓ cup of the sugar and salt in top of double boiler. Add beaten egg yolks and molasses and milk. Cook over hot water until mixture coats a silver spoon. Cool until mixture is the consistency of unbeaten egg whites. Beat egg whites until stiff. Beat in remaining ⅓ cup of sugar. Fold in gelatine mixture. Fold in whipped cream. Pour into pie shell. Chill until firm. Makes one 9-inch pie.

Strawberry Gelatin Pie

1½ cups strawberries
½ cup sugar, divided
1 package strawberry-flavored gelatin
1 cup hot water

3 eggs, separated
¼ teaspoon salt
1 9-inch baked crumb pie shell
½ cup heavy cream, whipped

Wash and hull berries. Place in a bowl and cut through with a knife several times. Sprinkle ¼ cup of the sugar over berries and let stand 30 minutes. Dissolve gelatin in hot water. Beat egg yolks slightly in top of a double boiler. Drain ¼ cup juice from strawberries and combine with egg yolks. Cook over hot water, stirring constantly, until thickened. Remove from heat and stir in gelatin. Chill until slightly thickened. Fold in strawberries. Beat egg whites until stiff. Gradually beat in salt and ¼ cup of sugar. Fold into gelatin mixture. Pour into graham cracker pie shell. Chill until firm. Garnish with whipped cream before serving. Makes one 9-inch pie.

Diamond Walnuts

Cranberry Chiffon Pie

1½ envelopes unflavored
   gelatine
2 tablespoons water
1 cup sugar, divided
1 cup canned whole
   cranberry sauce

2 egg whites
¼ teaspoon cream of tartar
⅛ teaspoon salt
1 cup heavy cream
1 baked Spicy Walnut
   Meringue Shell

Soften gelatine in water. Add 2/3 cup of the sugar and cranberry sauce. Heat mixture to boiling, stirring constantly. Remove and chill until mixture begins to thicken. Beat egg whites to soft peaks with cream of tartar and salt. Beat in remaining 1/3 cup sugar to form meringue. Beat cream stiff. Fold meringue and cream into cranberry filling. Turn into shell. Chill until firm. Garnish with walnut halves and whole cranberries if desired. Makes 6 to 8 servings.

Chocolate Nesselrode Pie

3 eggs, separated
1½ cups milk
¼ teaspoon salt
⅔ cup sugar, divided
1 envelope unflavored gelatine
2 tablespoons margarine
2 tablespoons finely chopped citron

3 tablespoons chopped almonds
¼ cup chopped maraschino cherries
1 teaspoon maraschino cherry juice
2 tablespoons rum flavoring
½ cup heavy cream, whipped
1 9-inch baked pie shell
Shaved sweet chocolate

Combine slightly beaten egg yolks, milk, salt, ⅓ cup of the sugar and gelatine in the top of a double boiler. Cook over hot water, stirring constantly, until mixture coats a silver spoon. Remove from heat and stir in margarine. Chill until mixture begins to thicken. Fold in citron, almonds, cherries, cherry juice and rum flavoring. Beat egg whites until stiff; beat in remaining ⅓ cup of the sugar. Fold into custard mixture. Fold in whipped cream. Pour into a baked pie shell. Chill until firm. Before serving sprinkle chocolate over top of pie. Makes one 9-inch pie.

Butterscotch Fluff Pie

1 cup sifted all-purpose
  flour
½ teaspoon salt
⅓ cup shortening
½ cup rolled oats (quick or
  old fashioned, uncooked)
4 to 5 tablespoons cold water
1 envelope unflavored
  gelatine

¼ cup cold water
½ teaspoon salt
1½ cups milk
2 eggs, separated
1 package (6-ounces)
  butterscotch pieces
½ cup heavy cream
2 tablespoons sugar
Toasted coconut

Sift together flour and salt into bowl. Cut in shortening until mixture resembles coarse crumbs; stir in oats. Add water, a tablespoon at a time, mixing with a fork until pastry can be formed into a ball. Turn out on lightly floured board or canvas. Roll out to form 13-inch circle. Fit pastry loosely into 9-inch pie plate. Turn edge under and flute. Prick bottom and sides with a fork. Bake in hot oven (425°F.) 12 to 15 minutes. Cool.

Soften gelatine in cold water. Place salt, milk, egg yolks and butterscotch pieces in top of double boiler. Cook over hot water until butterscotch pieces are melted and mixture thickens, stirring frequently. Add softened gelatine and stir until dissolved. Cool until mixture begins to thicken. Beat egg whites until stiff and glossy. Fold cooled gelatine mixture into egg whites. Whip cream until frothy; gradually add sugar, whipping until stiff. Fold into butterscotch mixture. Pour into pie crust; chill until set. Decorate with toasted coconut. Makes one 9-inch pie.

The Quaker Oats Company

Eggnog Nesselrode Pie

2 envelopes unflavored
   gelatine
¼ cup sugar
1 quart commercially
   prepared eggnog
2 teaspoons rum flavoring

1 cup heavy cream,
   whipped
⅓ cup chopped maraschino
   cherries
⅓ cup chopped nuts
1 10-inch baked pie shell

Combine gelatine and sugar in saucepan. Stir in 1 cup of the cold eggnog. Place over low heat, stirring constantly until gelatine and sugar are dissolved, about 3-5 minutes. Remove from heat; stir in rum flavoring and remaining eggnog. Chill until slightly thicker than the consistency of unbeaten egg white. Whip gelatine mixture until light and fluffy; fold in whipped cream. Fold in maraschino cherries and nuts. Turn into baked pie shell; chill until firm. If desired, garnish with additional whipped cream, pieces of maraschino cherry and citron "holly" leaves. Makes one 10-inch pie.

Knox Gelatine

Pumpkin Chiffon Pie

1 envelope unflavored gelatine
¼ cup cold water
1½ cups cooked or canned strained pumpkin
1 tablespoon grated lemon rind
½ cup brown sugar, firmly packed
3 eggs, separated

1 tablespoon cinnamon
½ teaspoon ginger
½ teaspoon mace
¼ teaspoon allspice
½ teaspoon salt
½ cup evaporated milk
2 tablespoons margarine
⅓ cup granulated sugar
1 9-inch baked pie shell

Soften gelatine in cold water. Combine remaining ingredients, except egg whites, granulated sugar and pie shell in top of a double boiler. Cook over boiling water about 10 minutes. Add gelatine and stir until dissolved. Remove from heat and chill until mixture begins to set. Beat egg whites until stiff; beat sugar in gradually. Fold into pumpkin mixture and pour into pie shell. Chill until firm. Just before serving, top with whipped cream. Makes one 9-inch pie.

Peach Chiffon Pie

1 envelope unflavored gelatine
⅓ cup sugar
⅛ teaspoon salt
1 tablespoon flour
1 No. 2½ can peach slices
3 tablespoons lemon juice

½ teaspoon grated lemon rind
1 cup evaporated milk, chilled
1 10-inch baked pie shell or
1 10-inch chocolate cookie crust

Combine in a small saucepan gelatine, sugar, salt and flour. Drain peaches; add 1½ cups of the peach syrup to sugar mixture. Cook, stirring constantly, until mixture thickens. Remove from heat and add lemon juice and rind. Chill until mixture is consistency of unbeaten egg whites. Beat with a rotary beater until fluffy. Whip chilled evaporated milk until it is the consistency of whipped cream. Fold the gelatine mixture into the whipped milk. Reserve eleven peach slices to garnish top of pie; fold remaining peach slices into gelatine mixture. Pour custard into pie shell. Chill until firm. Garnish top of pie with remaining peach slices. Makes one 10-inch pie.

Brazil Nut Black Bottom Pie

1½ cups ground Brazil nuts
3 tablespoons sugar
1 envelope unflavored gelatine
¼ cup cold water
⅔ cup sugar, divided
1 tablespoon cornstarch

4 eggs, separated
2 cups milk, scalded
1 package semi-sweet chocolate pieces
1 teaspoon vanilla
¼ teaspoon salt

Mix together Brazil nuts and 3 tablespoons sugar. Press this mixture with the back of a tablespoon against the bottom and sides of a 10-inch pie plate. Bake in a hot oven (400° F) 8 minutes, or until lightly browned. Cool. Soften gelatine in cold water. Combine ⅓ cup of the sugar and cornstarch. Beat egg yolks slightly; slowly add scalded milk. Stir in sugar mixture. Cook in double boiler, stirring constantly, until mixture is slightly thickened. To 1 cup custard, add semi-sweet chocolate pieces. Stir until chocolate is melted; set aside. To remaining custard, add softened gelatine. Stir until gelatine is dissolved, add vanilla. Cool. Beat egg whites until stiff; gradually beat in salt and remaining ⅓ cup of sugar. Fold in custard-gelatine mixture. Turn chocolate mixture into Brazil nut pie shell. Spoon gelatine mixture over chocolate layer and chill until firm. Garnish with whipped cream, maraschino cherries and Brazil nut slices. Makes one 10-inch pie.

Nesselrode Pie

1 envelope unflavored gelatine
1½ cups milk, divided
3 eggs, separated
⅓ cup mixed candied fruit
2 tablespoons ground almonds

1 cup crushed macaroons
⅛ teaspoon salt
2 tablespoons brandy flavoring
1 teaspoon vanilla
⅓ cup sugar
1 9-inch baked pie shell

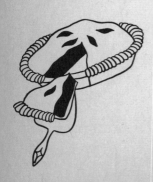

Soften gelatine in ¼ cup of the milk. Scald remaining milk in top of double boiler. Beat egg yolks slightly. Stir in hot milk, a little at a time; return to double boiler and add gelatine mixture. Cook over hot water, stirring occasionally, until mixture coats a silver spoon. Stir in candied fruit, almonds, macaroons, salt and flavorings. Cool mixture until thickened but not set. Beat egg whites until stiff and gradually beat in sugar until mixture is thick. Fold in gelatine mixture. Pour into pie shell and chill until firm. Makes one 9-inch pie.

Banana Bavarian Pie

½ cup melted butter or
margarine
2 cups crushed chocolate
cookie crumbs
1 envelope unflavored gelatine
¼ cup cold water

2 egg whites
1½ cups mashed bananas
3 tablespoons lemon juice
½ cup sugar
⅛ teaspoon salt
¾ cup heavy cream, whipped

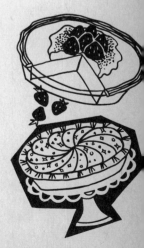

Combine butter and cookie crumbs. Reserve ⅓ cup of this
mixture. Press remaining cookie mixture into bottom and sides
of a 9-inch pie pan. Soften gelatine in cold water; dissolve over
hot water. Beat egg whites until stiff; add gelatine slowly, beating
until mixture stands in peaks. Combine bananas, lemon juice,
sugar and salt. Fold in egg whites and whipped cream. Pour mixture into chocolate cookie crust. Sprinkle reserved crumbs over
top of pie. Chill until firm. Makes one 9-inch pie.

Knox Gelatine

No-Bake Cheese Pie

1 envelope unflavored gelatine
½ cup sugar
⅛ teaspoon salt
1 cup milk
2 packages (8-ounces each) cream cheese

1 teaspoon lemon rind
1 tablespoon lemon juice
1 cup heavy cream, whipped
1 9-inch graham cracker crumb crust

Mix together gelatine, sugar and salt in saucepan. Stir in milk. Place over low heat, stirring constantly, until gelatine is dissolved, about 3 minutes. Remove from heat. Cool.

Beat cream cheese, lemon rind and lemon juice together on high speed of electric mixer. Gradually beat in gelatine mixture. Chill until mixture mounds, about 15 minutes. Fold in whipped cream. Turn into crumb shell. Chill until firm. If desired, garnish with graham cracker crumbs. Makes one 9-inch pie.

White Christmas Pie

1 envelope unflavored gelatine
1 cup sugar, divided
¼ cup flour
½ teaspoon salt
1¾ cups milk

¾ teaspoon vanilla
¼ teaspoon almond extract
½ cup heavy cream, whipped
3 egg whites
1 cup moist shredded coconut
1 9-inch baked pie shell

Combine gelatine, ½ cup of the sugar, flour and salt in a
saucepan. Stir in milk. Cook over low heat, stirring until it comes
to a full boil. Remove from heat. Cool. When partially set, beat
with a rotary beater until smooth. Blend in vanilla and almond
extract. Fold in cream. Beat egg whites until foamy. Gradually
beat in remaining sugar until mixture stands in stiff peaks. Fold
into gelatine mixture. Fold in coconut. Pile into pie shell. Chill
until set. Makes one 9-inch pie.

Grape Chiffon Pie

1 envelope unflavored gelatine
¼ cup cold water
1 cup grape juice
¼ cup sugar

1 tablespoon lemon juice
⅛ teaspoon salt
1 cup heavy cream, whipped
1 8-inch graham cracker
  crust

Soften gelatine in cold water; dissolve over hot water.
Combine grape juice, sugar, lemon juice and salt and stir until
sugar is dissolved. Add gelatine and stir well. Chill until mixture is the consistency of unbeaten egg whites. Fold in whipped
cream. Pour into cracker crust. Chill until firm. Makes one
8-inch pie.

Cream Pies

From pie in the sky to pie in your eye, these are the cream of the crop, Pop, you'll eat 'em 'till you drop!

Chocolate Polka Dot Pie

1 envelope unflavored gelatine
⅓ cup sugar, divided
1 tablespoon cornstarch
2¼ cups milk
3 eggs, separated

1 package semi-sweet chocolate
1 teaspoon vanilla
¼ teaspoon salt
½ cup heavy cream, whipped
1 10-inch baked pie shell

Combine gelatine, ⅓ cup of the sugar and cornstarch in top of double boiler. Stir in milk. Place over boiling water and stir until gelatine and sugar are dissolved. Beat egg yolks slightly; add small amount of hot mixture, return to double boiler and cook, stirring constantly, until thickened. To 1 cup of the gelatine mixture add ¾ package semi-sweet chocolate morsels; stir until chocolate is melted; set aside. To remaining custard add vanilla. Chill until the consistency of unbeaten egg white. Beat egg whites until stiff; gradually beat in salt and remaining ⅓ cup of sugar. Fold into vanilla-gelatine mixture. Fold in whipped cream. Pour chocolate mixture into baked pie shell. Spoon vanilla custard mixture over chocolate layer; chill until firm. Place remaining chocolate morsels upside down over pie to resemble polka dots. Makes one 10-inch pie.

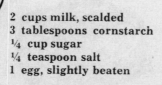

Peanut Brittle Pie

2 cups milk, scalded
3 tablespoons cornstarch
¼ cup sugar
¼ teaspoon salt
1 egg, slightly beaten

⅔ cup finely crushed peanut brittle, divided
1 teaspoon vanilla
1 9-inch baked graham cracker pie shell

Stir milk into combined cornstarch, sugar, salt and egg. Add ⅓ cup peanut brittle. Cook over hot water until thick, stirring frequently. Cool and add vanilla. Pour into pie shell. Sprinkle remaining peanut brittle over top of pie and chill well before serving. Makes one 9-inch pie.

Lemon Meringue Pie

1 package lemon pudding
  and pie filling mix
½ cup sugar
2 cups water

2 egg yolks
1 8- or 9-inch baked pie shell
2 egg whites
4 tablespoons sugar

Combine pie filling mix, ½ cup sugar and ¼ cup of the water in saucepan. Add egg yolks and blend well. Then add remaining 1¾ cups water. Cook and stir until mixture comes to a *full* boil and is thickened—about 5 minutes. Remove from heat. Cool only about 5 minutes, stirring once or twice. Pour into pie shell.

Beat egg whites until foamy throughout. Add 4 tablespoons sugar, 2 tablespoons at a time, beating after each addition until sugar is blended. Then continue beating until meringue will stand in peaks. Spread over pie filling. Bake in hot oven (425° F) 5 to 10 minutes, or until meringue is delicately browned. Makes one 8- or 9-inch pie.

Jell-o Pudding and Pie Filling

Grape Cream Pie

½ cup sugar
6 tablespoons cornstarch
¼ teaspoon salt
1 tablespoon grated
lemon rind

½ teaspoon cinnamon
2½ cups grape juice
1 tablespoon lemon juice
1 9-inch baked pie shell
½ cup heavy cream, whipped

Combine sugar, cornstarch, salt, lemon rind and cinnamon in a saucepan. Stir in grape juice and cook, over low heat, stirring constantly until thick. Add lemon juice. Cool and chill until very thick. Spoon mixture into pie shell and chill. Top with whipped cream. Makes one 9-inch pie.

Peach Cream Pie

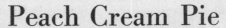

1 package vanilla
pudding mix
1¾ cups milk
1 egg, separated
1 tablespoon margarine

½ teaspoon almond extract
1 9-inch baked pie shell
8 peach halves
2 tablespoons sugar
Slivered almonds

Combine pudding mix, milk and egg yolk and cook according to directions on package. Stir in margarine and almond extract. Cool 5 minutes, stirring occasionally. Pour into pie shell. Slice 2 peach halves and arrange slices on top of pie. Arrange 6 peach halves on top of filling. Beat egg whites until stiff. Slowly beat in sugar until mixture is smooth and glossy. Fill centers of peach halves with a spoonful of the egg white mixture. Stick almond slivers in the egg white. Bake in a hot oven (425° F) about 5 minutes or until delicately browned. Makes one 9-inch pie.

Lemon Fluff Pie

4 eggs, separated
1⅓ cups sugar, divided
¼ teaspoon nutmeg
¼ cup lemon juice
2 teaspoons grated lemon rind
1 9-inch baked pie shell
½ cup coconut

Beat egg yolks in top of double boiler until thick and lemon colored. Add ⅔ cup sugar, gradually, beating well after each addition. Cook over hot water until mixture begins to thicken around sides of pan, about 5 to 7 minutes. Blend in nutmeg, lemon juice and lemon rind. Continue cooking until thick, about 10 minutes, stirring constantly. Beat egg whites until foamy. Add remaining ⅔ cup sugar gradually, beating well after each addition. Continue beating until egg whites stand in heavy peaks when beater is raised. Blend ⅓ of this meringue into lemon mixture. Cool. Turn into pie shell. Fold coconut into remaining meringue. Spread on top of filling. Bake in a hot oven (425° F) 5 to 10 minutes, or until lightly browned. Makes one 9-inch pie.

Coconut Crunch Pie

3 eggs, separated
1¼ cups sugar
1 teaspoon salt
½ cup milk
2 tablespoons soft butter or margarine
½ teaspoon almond extract
¼ teaspoon lemon extract
1 cup shredded coconut
1 9-inch unbaked pie shell

Beat egg yolks well. Add sugar and salt and mix well. Stir in milk, butter, and extracts. Fold in coconut. Beat egg whites until stiff but not dry. Fold into egg yolk mixture. Pour into pie shell. Bake in a moderate oven (350° F) 35 to 40 minutes or until a knife inserted in center comes out clean. Makes one 9-inch pie.

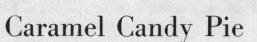

Caramel Candy Pie

1 envelope unflavored gelatine
¼ cup cold water
½ pound candy caramels
½ cup milk, divided
1 cup heavy cream, whipped
1 9-inch baked pie shell

Soften gelatine in cold water. Combine caramels and ¼ cup of the milk in top of a double boiler. Cook over boiling water until caramels melt. Stir until smooth. Add softened gelatine and stir until dissolved. Remove from heat and stir in ¼ cup of cold milk. Chill until the consistency of unbeaten egg whites. Add caramel mixture to whipped cream and beat with a rotary beater until well blended. Turn into baked pie shell. Chill until firm. Makes one 9-inch pie.

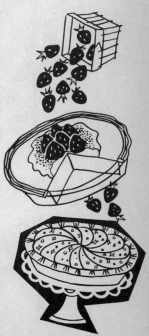

Mississippi Pecan Pie

3 eggs, slightly beaten   1 teaspoon vanilla
¼ cup sugar   ⅔ cup whole pecans
1¼ cups corn syrup   1 9-inch unbaked pie shell
¼ teaspoon salt

    Combine all ingredients, except pie shell, in order listed. Blend well and pour into pie shell. Bake in a hot oven (450° F) 10 minutes; reduce temperature to 325° F and bake 30 minutes or until a silver knife, inserted in the center, comes out clean. Makes one 9-inch pie.

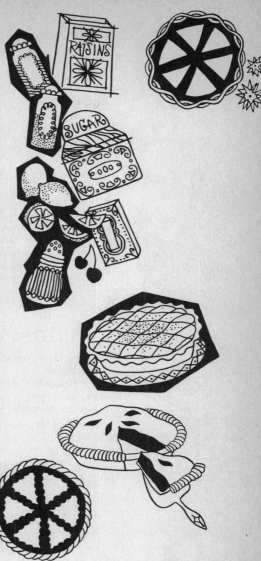

Mocha Chocolate Pie

1 package chocolate
  pudding mix
4 teaspoons instant coffee

1½ cups milk
½ cup heavy cream, whipped
1 8-inch baked pie shell

Combine pudding mix, instant coffee and milk in a saucepan according to directions on package. Cook and stir over medium heat until mixture comes to a full boil. Remove from heat. Cool about 5 minutes, stirring once or twice. Fold in whipped cream. Pour into pie shell. Chill well before serving. If desired, garnish with a border of whipped cream and chopped nuts. Makes one 8-inch pie.

Peanut Scotch Pie

½ cup sugar
¾ cup brown sugar, firmly packed
¼ cup sifted flour
½ teaspoon salt
3 eggs, separated
2 cups milk

1 tablespoon butter or margarine
3 tablespoons peanut butter
1 9-inch baked pie shell
6 tablespoons sugar
¼ cup finely chopped peanuts

Combine sugar, brown sugar, flour and salt in top of a double boiler. Stir in egg yolks, milk and butter. Cook over boiling water, stirring occasionally, until thickened. Remove from heat. Add peanut butter and blend well. Cover and cool. Pour into baked pie shell. Beat egg whites until foamy. Gradually beat in 6 tablespoons sugar until mixture stands in stiff peaks. Spread meringue over filling in pie shell. Sprinkle peanuts over top of meringue. Bake in a hot oven (425° F) 5 to 10 minutes. or until golden brown. Makes one 9-inch pie.

Pennsylvania Cheese Pie

2 teaspoons cornstarch
⅔ cup sugar
1 cup cottage cheese, riced
2 eggs, separated
2 tablespoons milk

⅛ teaspoon salt
1 tablespoon grated lemon rind
1 9-inch unbaked pie shell

Mix cornstarch and sugar; add cottage cheese, egg yolks, milk, salt and lemon rind and blend well. Fold in stiffly beaten egg whites and pour into pie shell. Bake in a hot oven (450° F) 10 minutes. Reduce temperature to 325° F and continue baking 25 to 30 minutes. Makes one 9-inch pie.

Pineapple Cheese Pie

1 No. 2 can crushed pineapple
2 tablespoons cornstarch
2 teaspoons cold water
½ pound creamy cottage cheese
¼ cup butter or margarine

1 cup sugar
2 eggs, unbeaten
½ cup sifted flour
¾ cup milk
1 teaspoon vanilla
1 9-inch unbaked pie shell

Cook pineapple in a saucepan over low heat 5 minutes. Combine cornstarch and water; stir into pineapple and cook until clear. Cool. Combine cheese and butter; add sugar gradually, beating until light and fluffy. Add eggs singly, beating well after each addition. Add flour alternately with combined milk and vanilla. Pour pineapple mixture into unbaked pie shell. Top with cheese mixture. Bake in a hot oven (450° F) 10 minutes; reduce temperature to 350° F and continue baking 30 minutes. Makes one 9-inch pie.

Fresh Peach Pie

1 recipe pastry
⅔ cup sugar
¾ teaspoon nutmeg
¼ teaspoon salt
2 teaspoons cornstarch
1 egg yolk, slightly beaten

3 cups peeled, sliced peaches
2½ tablespoons butter or
   margarine, melted
2 tablespoons evaporated
   milk
2 teaspoons lemon juice

Line an 8-inch pie plate with one-half the pastry. Blend together sugar, nutmeg, salt and cornstarch. Blend in egg yolk. Add remaining ingredients and mix thoroughly. Pour into pastry-lined pie plate. Cover with lattice top. Bake in a hot oven (450° F) 15 minutes; reduce temperature to 350° F and continue baking 35 minutes. Makes one 8-inch pie.

Mincemeat Custard Pie

1½ cups prepared
   mincement
1 9-inch unbaked pie shell
3 eggs, slightly beaten

¼ cup sugar
¼ teaspoon salt
2 cups milk
Nutmeg

Spread mincemeat in the pie shell. Combine eggs, sugar, salt and milk and mix well. Pour over mincemeat. Sprinkle with nutmeg. Bake in a very hot oven (450° F) 15 minutes; reduce heat to moderate 350° F and bake 30 minutes, or until a knife inserted in the center comes out clean. Serve warm. Makes one 9-inch pie.

The Borden Company

Pecan Crumb Pie

½ cup eggs (about 3)
1 cup sugar, divided
2 cups graham cracker crumbs
¼ cup flour
1 teaspoon baking powder

½ cup chopped pecans
2 tablespoons butter or margarine, melted
1 teaspoon vanilla
¼ cup apricot jam
½ cup heavy cream, whipped

Beat eggs until very light with ½ cup of the sugar. Combine remaining sugar with crumbs, flour, baking powder and pecans. Add butter, vanilla and beaten eggs and mix lightly. Pour into a buttered 9-inch pie plate. Bake in a moderate oven (350° F) 30 to 35 minutes. Cool. Serve garnished with apricot jam and cream. Makes one 9-inch pie.

Perfect Pie

4 eggs, separated
¼ teaspoon cream of tartar
1½ cups sugar, divided
3 tablespoons lemon juice
1 tablespoon grated lemon rind
⅛ teaspoon salt
1 pint heavy cream

Beat egg whites and cream of tartar until stiff. Add 1 cup of the sugar, 1 tablespoon at a time, beating well after each addition. Continue beating until stiff and glossy. Line bottom and sides of a 9-inch pie plate with this mixture. Bake in a low oven (275° F) about 1 hour or until lightly browned. Cool. Beat egg yolks slightly. Stir in remaining sugar, lemon juice, lemon rind and salt. Cook in top of double boiler, over boiling water, until very thick. Remove from heat and cool. Whip 1 cup of the cream until stiff. Fold into cooked egg mixture. Fill meringue shell. Chill in refrigerator 24 hours before serving. Just before serving top with 1 cup cream, whipped. Makes one 9-inch pie.

Silky Chocolate Pie

½ cup butter
¾ cup sugar
1 square unsweetened chocolate, melted and cooled
1 teaspoon vanilla
2 eggs
1 8-inch baked pie shell

Cream butter. Add sugar gradually and cream well. Blend in chocolate and vanilla. Add eggs, one at a time, and beat 5 minutes with a rotary beater after each addition. Turn into baked pie shell and chill 1 to 2 hours before serving. Top with whipped cream before serving if desired. Makes one 8-inch pie.

Graham Cracker Butterscotch Pie

2 cups milk, divided
1 cup dark brown sugar, firmly packed
2 egg yolks
3 tablespoons cornstarch
3 tablespoons butter or margarine
1 9-inch graham cracker pie crust
½ cup whipped cream

Heat ½ cup of the milk and the brown sugar in the top part of a double boiler until sugar is dissolved. Beat egg yolks well, add cornstarch and remaining 1½ cups of milk. Add mixture to milk and sugar in top of double boiler. Cook over hot water until mixture is thickened, then cook 5 minutes longer, stirring constantly. Remove from heat and stir in butter. Pour into graham cracker lined pie plate and chill in refrigerator. Serve topped with whipped cream. Makes one 9-inch pie.

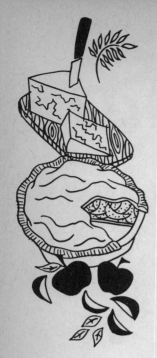

Creamy Lemon Pie

1 cup sugar
½ teaspoon salt
¼ cup flour
1 cup milk
2 eggs, separated

Rind and juice of 1 lemon
⅓ cup butter or margarine
1 8-inch baked pie shell
4 tablespoons sugar

Combine sugar, salt and flour in the top of a double boiler. Mix well and stir in milk. Cook over very low heat, stirring constantly, until thickened. Beat egg yolks. Pour the hot mixture slowly over egg yolks and mix well. Return mixture to double boiler. Cook over hot water about 3 minutes. Remove from heat. Add lemon juice and rind and butter. Cool, stirring occasionally. Pour into baked pie shell. Beat egg whites until stiff but not dry. Gradually beat in sugar until mixture stands in peaks. Pile on top of lemon filling in pie shell. Bake in a hot oven (425° F) 5 to 10 minutes, or until lightly browned. Makes one 8-inch pie.

Apple Custard Pie

3 eggs
¼ cup sugar
¼ teaspoon salt
Grated rind of ½ lemon

1 cup grated raw apple
2 cups milk, scalded
1 9-inch unbaked pie shell
Cinnamon

Beat eggs slightly, add sugar, salt, lemon rind and apple. Add milk and strain, forcing the apple through the sieve. Pour into unbaked pie shell. Sprinkle a little cinnamon on the top. Bake in a hot oven (400° F) 10 minutes, reduce the temperature to 300° F and continue baking 30 to 45 minutes or until a silver knife inserted in the center comes out clean. Makes one 9-inch pie.

Golden Nugget Orange Pie

⅓ cup sugar
4 tablespoons cornstarch
1¼ cups orange juice
1 cup pineapple juice
3 eggs, separated

1½ cups pineapple pieces, drained
1 tablespoon butter or margarine
1 9-inch baked pie shell
6 tablespoons sugar

Combine sugar, cornstarch, orange juice, and pineapple juice in a saucepan. Mix until smooth. Cook over medium heat, stirring constantly, until thick and clear. Stir a little of the hot mixture into the beaten egg yolks and return to saucepan. Cook over very low heat, and cook about 2 minutes, stirring constantly. Remove from heat. Stir in pineapple pieces and butter. Cover and cool. Pour into baked shell. Beat egg whites until foamy. Gradually beat in sugar until stiff. Spread meringue over filling. Bake in a hot oven (425° F) 5 to 10 minutes. Makes one 9-inch pie.

Apricot Whip Pie

1 cup puréed cooked dried
   apricots
¼ teaspoon salt
¾ cup sugar
2 egg whites

¼ teaspoon almond extract
1 tablespoon lemon juice
1 8-inch oatmeal pie crust
Apricot halves, cooked

Place apricots, salt, sugar, unbeaten egg whites, extract
and lemon juice in a large bowl. Beat with rotary beater until
light and fluffy and stiff enough to stand in peaks. Heap into
oatmeal pie crust. Chill. Garnish with apricot halves. Makes
one 8-inch pie.

Deep South Pie

1 cup cooked rice
¼ cup butter or margarine
¾ cup molasses
1 cup sugar
2 eggs, beaten

¼ teaspoon salt
1 teaspoon vanilla
1 9-inch unbaked pie shell
1 cup whole pecans

Cook rice until very soft (at least twice as long as customary).
Drain and mash with a fork. Melt butter in a large saucepan.
Stir in molasses, sugar, eggs, salt, vanilla and rice and pour into
pie shell. Sprinkle pecans evenly over the top. Bake in a moderate oven (375° F) 50 minutes. Cool before serving. Makes one
9-inch pie.

Sweet Potato Mince Pie

1 cup cooked, mashed
   sweet potatoes
1 cup evaporated milk
¼ cup brown sugar, packed
1 egg, slightly beaten
½ teaspoon salt
¼ teaspoon cinnamon

¼ teaspoon ginger
1 teaspoon grated lemon rind
1½ tablespoons margarine,
   melted
1 package mincemeat
1 9-inch unbaked pie shell

Combine sweet potatoes, milk, sugar, egg, seasonings, rind and margarine; cook over low heat 3 minutes, stirring constantly. Prepare mincemeat according to directions on package; spread on bottom of pastry in pie dish; pour potato mixture over mincemeat. Bake in hot oven (450° F) 15 minutes; reduce temperature to 350° F and continue baking 25 to 30 minutes or until a silver knife comes out clean when inserted in the center. Makes one 9-inch pie.

Chocolate Brownie Pie

2 squares unsweetened
   chocolate
2 tablespoons butter or
   margarine
3 eggs

½ cup sugar
¾ cup dark corn syrup
¾ cup pecan halves
1 9-inch unbaked pie shell

Melt chocolate and butter together over hot water. Beat eggs thoroughly. Beat in sugar, chocolate mixture and corn syrup. Stir in pecan halves. Pour mixture into pastry lined pie dish. Bake in a moderate oven (375° F) 40 to 50 minutes, just until pie is set. Makes one 9-inch pie.

Best Foods, Inc.

Peanut Butter Pie

1 cup light or dark corn
   syrup
1 cup sugar
3 eggs, slightly beaten

½ teaspoon vanilla
⅓ cup creamy or chunk
   style peanut butter
1 unbaked (9-inch) pastry
   shell

Blend corn syrup, sugar, eggs, vanilla and peanut butter in a bowl. Pour into unbaked pastry shell. Bake in hot oven (400°F.) for 15 minutes. Reduce heat to 350°F. and bake 30 to 35 minutes longer. (Filling should appear slightly less set in center than around edge.)

103

Custard Pie with Crispy Crust

4 eggs, slightly beaten
2½ cups milk
½ cup sugar
1 teaspoon vanilla

½ teaspoon salt
⅛ teaspoon nutmeg
1 9-inch baked pie shell

Combine eggs, milk, sugar, vanilla, salt and nutmeg and blend well. Strain into an oiled 9-inch pie pan. Place pan in a shallow pan of hot water. Bake in a moderate oven (350° F) about 35 minutes. Cool to room temperature. Loosen custard from sides of pan with a spatula. Shake gently to loosen from pan. Slide custard quickly into baked pie shell. Makes one 9-inch pie.

Shoo-Fly Pie

1 cup molasses
1 cup boiling water
1 teaspoon baking soda
3 cups sifted flour

1 cup sugar
½ cup butter
1 9-inch unbaked pie shell

Combine molasses, water and baking soda; bring to a boil. Boil 1 minute or until light in color. Sift together flour and sugar. Cut in butter with 2 knives or a pastry blender, to a crumb consistency. Pour molasses mixture into pastry shell; top with crumb mixture. Bake in a hot oven (425° F) 40 minutes. Cool. Makes one 9-inch pie.

Sour Cream Raisin Pie

2 tablespoons cornstarch
1 cup sugar, divided
¼ teaspoon salt
¼ teaspoon cinnamon
½ teaspoon nutmeg

2 eggs, separated
1 cup sour cream
1 cup raisins
1½ teaspoons lemon juice
1 9-inch baked pie shell

In the top of a double boiler mix together cornstarch, ¾ cup of the sugar, salt, cinnamon and nutmeg. Add egg yolks and mix well. Add sour cream. Cook over hot water until thick, stirring constantly. Stir in raisins and lemon juice. Cool. Pour into baked pie shell. Beat egg whites until stiff. Gradually beat in the remaining ¼ cup of sugar. Spread over filling. Bake in a hot oven (425° F) 5 to 10 minutes, or until delicately browned. Makes one 9-inch pie.

Chocolate Pie

1 cup sugar
1 teaspoon salt
3½ tablespoons cornstarch
3 cups milk
3 squares unsweetened
  chocolate

3 eggs, separated
1 tablespoon butter or
  margarine
1 teaspoon vanilla
1 9-inch baked pie shell
6 tablespoons sugar

Beat the yolks until light and thick. Combine sugar, salt, cornstarch in top of double boiler. Stir in the milk and chocolate. Cook over boiling water, stirring, until thick. Cover and cook for 10 more minutes. Beat egg yolks. Pour hot mixture slowly over egg yolks and mix well. Return to double boiler and cook, stirring constantly, about 2 minutes. Add butter and vanilla. Cool. Pour into baked pie shell. Beat egg whites until stiff but not dry. Add sugar gradually, beating until mixture stands in peaks. Cover top of chocolate with meringue. Bake in a hot oven (425° F) 5 to 10 minutes or until lightly browned. Makes one 9-inch pie.

Baked Chocolate Sponge Pie

¼ cup butter or margarine
1 cup sugar, divided
3 tablespoons flour
6 tablespoons cocoa

3 eggs, separated
1 teaspoon vanilla
2 cups milk
1 9-inch unbaked pie shell

Cream together butter and ⅔ cup of the sugar. Stir in flour and cocoa. Add egg yolks separately, beating well after each addition. Stir in vanilla and milk. Beat egg whites until stiff. Gradually beat in remaining ⅓ cup of the sugar and continue beating until egg whites stand in peaks. Fold whites into chocolate mixture and turn into unbaked pie shell. Bake in a hot oven (425° F) 15 minutes, then reduce heat to low (325° F) and continue baking 30 minutes or until firm to the touch. Makes one 9-inch pie.

Fruit in Cream Pie

1 cup canned, sliced
  peaches, drained
½ cup chopped dates
½ cup quartered
  marshmallows
1½ cups sliced bananas

3 tablespoons lemon juice
3 tablespoons honey
½ cup heavy cream, whipped
1 9-inch baked pie shell
2 tablespoons crushed
  cheese crackers

Combine peaches, dates, marshmallows, bananas, lemon juice and honey. Chill thoroughly. Fold fruit mixture carefully into whipped cream. Turn into pie shell. Sprinkle with crushed cheese crackers. Chill until ready to serve. Makes one 9-inch pie.

Apricot Cottage Cheese Pie

2 cups mashed, cooked
  apricots
1 teaspoon lemon extract
¼ teaspoon almond extract
1 cup sugar, divided
1 9-inch unbaked pie shell

⅛ teaspoon salt
2 eggs, beaten
1 cup milk
1 teaspoon vanilla
1 cup cottage cheese

Combine apricots, lemon extract, almond extract and ½ cup of the sugar. Spread in bottom of pie shell. Bake in a hot oven (425° F) 10 minutes. Combine remaining sugar and salt with eggs and mix well. Add remaining ingredients. Pour mixture over apricots in pie shell. Reduce temperature to low 325° F and continue baking 50 minutes. Serve with whipped cream if desired. Makes one 9-inch pie.

Scotch Banana Pie

2 bananas
1 8-inch cornflake pie crust
1 package butterscotch
  pudding mix

1¾ cups milk
2 tablespoons margarine
⅓ cup chopped pecans

Slice one banana and arrange in bottom of cornflake pie crust. Prepare pudding with the milk according to directions on the package. When mixture comes to a full boil remove from heat and stir in margarine and pecans. Cool about 5 minutes, stirring occasionally. Pour into pie crust. Chill until firm. Just before serving garnish top with sliced banana and chopped nuts. Makes one 8-inch pie.

Prize-Winning
Lemon Meringue Pie

One 9-inch baked pie shell
7 tablespoons cornstarch
1⅓ cups sugar
¼ teaspoon salt
1½ cups hot water

3 egg yolks, beaten
½ cup lemon juice
1 teaspoon grated lemon rind
2 tablespoons butter or
margarine

Mix cornstarch, sugar and salt in a saucepan. Stir in hot water gradually and bring to a boil over direct heat. Cook for 8 to 10 minutes over medium heat, stirring constantly until thick and clear. Remove from the heat. Stir several spoonfuls of this hot mixture into the beaten egg yolks. Mix well. Pour egg yolks back into the saucepan. Bring to a boil then reduce heat and cook slowly for 4 to 5 minutes, stirring constantly. Remove from heat and gradually add lemon juice, rind and butter. Cool thoroughly, then pour into the cooled baked pie shell. Top with meringue: put the 3 egg whites (at room temperature) in a deep medium sized bowl. Add 1 tablespoon lemon juice. Beat until whites stand in soft peaks. Add 6 tablespoons sugar gradually, beating well after each addition. Beat until egg whites stand in firm glossy peaks. Spread over cooled filling, starting at the edges and working toward the center of the pie, attaching meringue securely to the edges of the crust. Bake at 350° F. for 15 to 20 minutes. Cool but do not refrigerate before serving.

Sunkist Growers

Coffee Meringue Pie

⅔ cup sugar
5 tablespoons cornstarch
½ teaspoon salt
1 cup milk
1½ cups strong coffee

2 eggs, separated
1 9-inch baked pie shell
⅛ teaspoon salt
4 tablespoons sugar

Mix sugar, cornstarch and salt in top part of double boiler. Add combined milk and coffee. Cook over direct heat, stirring constantly, until smooth and thick. Beat egg yolks slightly. Pour hot mixture slowly over egg yolks and mix well. Return to double boiler and cook over hot water about 5 minutes, stirring occasionally. Cool. Pour into baked pie shell. Beat egg whites with salt until stiff. Gradually beat in sugar and continue beating until mixture stands in peaks. Arrange on top of filling. Bake in a hot oven (425° F) 5 to 10 minutes or until lightly browned. Makes one 9-inch pie.

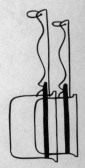

Old-South Butterscotch Pie

1¼ cups dark brown sugar, firmly packed
¼ teaspoon salt
2 tablespoons water
2 cups milk, divided
4½ tablespoons cornstarch
3 egg yolks, slightly beaten
2 tablespoons butter or margarine
½ teaspoon vanilla
1 9-inch baked pie shell
⅓ cup pecans, chopped
1 cup heavy cream, whipped

Combine brown sugar, salt and water in top of a double boiler. Cook over direct heat for 5 minutes. Blend ¼ cup of the milk with the cornstarch. Add the remaining milk and combine with the brown sugar mixture. Place over hot water and cook until thick and smooth, about 20 minutes, stirring occasionally. Stir a small amount of the hot mixture over the beaten egg yolks and mix well; return to double boiler and cook 5 minutes longer. Add butter and vanilla; remove from hot water and cool. Pour into baked shell and chill well. Before serving, sprinkle top with pecans and garnish with whipped cream. Makes one 9-inch pie.

Heavenly Chocolate Pie

1 cup sifted flour
¾ teaspoon salt, divided
⅓ cup shortening
3 to 4 tablespoons cold water
2 eggs, separated
½ teaspoon vinegar
¾ cup sugar, divided
1 package (6-ounces) semi-sweet chocolate morsels
¼ cup water
1 cup heavy cream
¼ teaspoon cinnamon

Combine flour and ½ teaspoon salt in mixing bowl. Cut in shortening until consistency of coarse meal. Sprinkle water, over mixture, tossing quickly and lightly with fork until dough is just moist enough to hold together. Roll out pastry and fit into a 9-inch pie plate. Flute edges and prick bottom with a fork. Bake in a very hot oven (450°F.) 12 minutes. Beat together egg whites, vinegar and remaining ¼ teaspoon salt until stiff but not dry. Gradually add ½ cup of the sugar and beat until very stiff. Spread meringue over bottom and up sides of baked shell. Bake in a moderate oven (325°F.) 15 to 18 minutes, or until lightly browned. Cool. Melt chocolate morsels over hot water. Beat together egg yolks and ¼ cup water until smooth. Beat in melted chocolate. Spread 3 tablespoons of chocolate mixture over cooled meringue. Chill remaining chocolate mixture until it begins to thicken. Beat together heavy cream, remaining ¼ cup sugar and cinnamon until thick. Spread ½ of the whipped cream mixture over chocolate layer in pie shell. Fold chilled chocolate mixture into remaining whipped cream. Spread over plain whipped cream in pie shell. Chill pie at least 4 hours before serving. Makes one 9-inch pie.

Nestle

Rainbow Ice Cream Pie

½ cup chopped mixed
   candied fruits
¼ cup chopped pecans
½ cup light corn syrup
¼ cup sugar
¼ cup orange juice
½ teaspoon rum flavoring
⅔ cup brown edge or
   vanilla wafer fine
   cookie crumbs

3 tablespoons melted
   butter
12 whole brown edge or
   vanilla wafer cookies
1 pint chocolate ice cream
1 pint vanilla ice cream
1 pint strawberry ice
   cream

Combine candied fruits, pecans, corn syrup, sugar and orange juice in a saucepan. Bring to a boil and simmer 1 minute. Remove from heat and stir in rum flavoring. Chill. Combine cookie crumbs and butter and blend well. Press mixture evenly over bottom of a 9-inch pie plate. Stand whole cookies upright around edge. Chill. Spoon chocolate ice cream into a layer in cookie crust and drizzle ¼ of the sauce over top. Repeat process using vanilla and strawberry ice cream and sauce. Freeze until serving time. Serve with remaining sauce. Makes one 9-inch pie.

National Dairy Council

Gingerbread Meringue Pie

3 tablespoons sugar
¼ cup molasses
¼ cup corn syrup
3 tablespoons shortening
1 teaspoon ginger
½ teaspoon cinnamon
Pinch of salt

½ cup boiling water
1 teaspoon soda
1¼ cups sifted flour
1 egg, well beaten
1 9-inch unbaked pie shell
2 egg whites
4 tablespoons sugar

Combine 3 tablespoons sugar, molasses, corn syrup, shorten-ing, ginger, cinnamon and salt. Combine water and soda and add to molasses mixture. Stir in flour. Beat together with rotary beater. Add egg, and beat again. Pour into shell. Bake in a moderate oven (375° F) until firm, about 40 minutes. Beat egg whites until stiff but not dry. Gradually beat in 4 tablespoons sugar until mixture stands in peaks. Cover pie with meringue and bake in a hot oven (425° F) 5 to 10 minutes or until browned. Makes one 9-inch pie.

Raisin Chocolate Pie

1 cup raisins
2¼ cups milk, scalded
½ teaspoon salt
1 cup sugar, divided
¼ cup cocoa

¼ cup cornstarch
2 eggs, separated
2 tablespoons cold water
2 teaspoons vanilla
1 9-inch baked pie shell

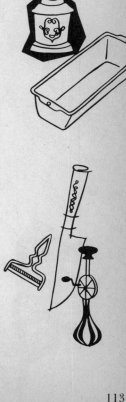

Boil raisins 5 minutes in water to cover; drain well and set aside. Scald milk in top of double boiler. Combine salt, ¾ cup sugar, cocoa and cornstarch and blend thoroughly. Add slowly to scalded milk, stirring to prevent lumping. Beat together egg yolks and water. Pour the hot mixture slowly over egg yolks and mix well. Return mixture to double boiler and cook over hot water until thick and clear, stirring occasionally. Remove from heat. Cool and fold in vanilla and raisins. Pour into baked pie shell. Beat egg whites until stiff but not dry. Add sugar gradually, beating until mixture stands in peaks. Pile over pie filling. Bake in a hot oven (425° F) 5 to 10 minutes or until meringue is lightly browned. Makes one 9-inch pie.

Yambilee Ice Cream Pie

¾ cup ginger snap crumbs
(about 12 2-inch
cookies)
2 tablespoons melted
butter or margarine
1 tablespoon sugar
11 2-inch ginger snaps
1 pint vanilla ice cream,
softened
¼ cup chopped pecans

3 cups mashed cooked
yams
¼ cup maple-blended
syrup
½ cup heavy cream
¼ teaspoon orange extract
1 tablespoon sugar
¼ teaspoon cinnamon
Pecans

Mix crumbs, butter and 1 tablespoon sugar; press into bottom of 9-inch pie plate. Place ginger snaps around edge of pie plate. Combine ice cream, chopped pecans, yams and syrup; blend thoroughly. Pour yam mixture into pie plate; freeze. Combine heavy cream, orange extract, 1 tablespoon sugar and cinnamon; whip until soft peaks form. Garnish frozen pie with whipped cream and pecans.

Note: If pie is very firm, let stand at room temperature 15 minutes before serving.

Louisiana Yam Commission

Never-Fail Lemon Meringue Pie

24 vanilla cookie wafers
1⅓ cups (15-ounce can)
sweetened condensed milk
½ cup lemon juice
1 teaspoon grated lemon rind

¼ teaspoon salt
2 eggs, separated
¼ teaspoon cream of tartar
4 tablespoons sugar

Line an 8-inch pie pan with vanilla wafers; crumble several of the wafers to fill spaces between cookies in bottom of pie pan. Pour sweetened condensed milk into mixing bowl; add lemon juice, rind, salt and egg yolks. Beat with a rotary beater until blended. Turn filling into pie shell. Add cream of tartar to egg whites and beat until stiff but not dry. Add sugar gradually, beating until mixture stands in peaks. Spread over lemon filling. Bake in a hot oven (425° F) 5 to 10 minutes or until lightly browned. Cool before serving. Makes one 8-inch pie.

The Borden Company

Eggnog Coconut Pie

1 package vanilla pudding
  and pie filling mix
1 tablespoon brandy

2 tablespoons rum extract
1 9-inch baked coconut
  pie crust

Prepare pudding mix as directed on package. Add brandy and rum extract. Cool about 5 minutes, stirring once or twice. Turn into coconut pie crust. Chill well before serving. Garnish with whipped cream, if desired. Makes one 9-inch pie.

Currant Pie

3 eggs, separated
1¼ cups brown sugar,
  firmly packed
½ teaspoon cinnamon
¼ teaspoon cloves

2 teaspoons butter
1 teaspoon vinegar
½ cup dried currants
¾ cup chopped walnuts
1 8-inch unbaked pie shell

Combine egg yolks, brown sugar, cinnamon, cloves and butter and beat until well blended. Stir in vinegar, currants and walnuts. Beat egg whites until stiff but not dry. Fold into fruit mixture. Pour into pie shell. Bake in a very hot oven (450° F) 10 minutes, reduce temperature to 325° F and bake 20 to 25 minutes. Makes one 8-inch pie.

Peaches and Cream Pie

1 No. 2½ can peach halves,
  drained
    or
5 fresh peaches, peeled and
  sliced
1 9-inch unbaked pie shell

2 eggs
1 cup sour cream
¼ cup honey
½ cup brown sugar, firmly
  packed
2 tablespoons flour

Arrange peach halves or slices in pie shell. Beat eggs slightly, add cream and honey and mix well. Pour over peaches. Blend together brown sugar and flour and sprinkle over egg mixture. Bake in a very hot oven (450° F) 15 minutes; reduce temperature to 350° F and bake 25 to 30 minutes. Makes one 9-inch pie.

Sweet Potato Pie

2 cups hot mashed sweet
  potatoes
1 cup evaporated milk
2 tablespoons brown sugar
1 cup hot water
¼ cup molasses

1 soda cracker, finely
  crushed
½ teaspoon ginger
½ teaspoon salt
2 tablespoons raisins
1 9-inch unbaked pie shell

Combine potatoes, milk, sugar, water and molasses. Blend together cracker crumbs, ginger and salt; add to potato mixture. Stir in raisins. Pour into unbaked pastry shell. Bake in a hot oven (450° F) 10 minutes; reduce temperature to 350° F and continue baking 25 minutes or until firm. Makes one 9-inch pie.

Lemon-Lime Meringue Pie

1¼ cups sugar, divided
1 tablespoon butter or
  margarine
1¾ cups water, divided
⅛ teaspoon salt
5 tablespoons cornstarch

2 eggs, separated
2½ tablespoons lime juice
2½ tablespoons lemon juice
Grated rind of 1 lemon
Grated rind of 1 lime
1 9-inch baked pie shell

Mix together 1 cup sugar, butter, 1½ cups of the water and salt in top of a double boiler. Cook over low heat until mixture boils. Mix cornstarch with remaining water, add to sugar syrup and cook over hot water 20 minutes. Beat egg yolks. Pour the hot mixture slowly into egg yolks and mix well. Return to double boiler and cook 3 minutes, stirring constantly. Remove from hot water and cool. Add fruit juices and rinds; blend well. When filling is cold, pour into baked pie shell. Beat egg whites until stiff but not dry. Add sugar gradually, beating until mixture stands in peaks. Pile on top of filling. Bake in a hot oven (425° F) 5 to 10 minutes or until lightly browned. Makes one 9-inch pie.

National Dairy Council

Pumpkin Pie

2 cups cooked or canned
   mashed pumpkin
½ cup firmly packed
   brown sugar
1 teaspoon salt
½ teaspoon cinnamon

½ teaspoon nutmeg
½ teaspoon ginger
¼ teaspoon cloves
3 eggs, slightly beaten
2 cups milk
1 9-inch unbaked pie shell

Combine pumpkin, sugar and seasonings. Blend in eggs and milk and mix well. Pour into unbaked pie shell. Bake in a hot oven (450° F) 10 minutes; reduce temperature to 350° F and continue baking 25 to 30 minutes or until knife inserted in center comes out clean. Serve with whipped cream if desired. Makes one 9-inch pie.

Chocolate Marshmallow Pie

2 squares unsweetened
   chocolate
2 tablespoons sugar
½ cup milk
12 marshmallows

1½ cups heavy cream,
   whipped
1 8-inch baked pie shell
½ cup toasted chopped
   almonds

Put chocolate, sugar, milk and marshmallows in top of a double boiler. Melt over hot water. Cool, stirring frequently. Fold in whipped cream. Pour into baked pie shell. Sprinkle with chopped almonds. Chill well before serving. Makes one 8-inch pie.

Lime Meringue Pie

4 tablespoons cornstarch
¾ cup sugar
¼ teaspoon salt
1¼ cups water
3 eggs, separated

1 tablespoon butter
2 teaspoons grated lime rind
5 tablespoons lime juice
1 8-inch baked pie shell
6 tablespoons sugar

Blend cornstarch, sugar and salt in top of a double boiler. Stir in water. Cook over direct heat, stirring constantly, until mixture is very thick and transparent. Beat egg yolks. Pour hot mixture slowly over egg yolks and mix well. Return to double boiler and cook over hot water 3 minutes, stirring constantly. Remove from heat. Stir in butter, lime rind and juice. Turn into baked pie shell. Beat egg whites until stiff but not dry. Add 6 tablespoons of sugar gradually, beating until mixture stands in peaks. Pile over pie filling. Bake in a hot oven (425° F) 5 to 10 minutes. Makes one 8-inch pie.

Peanut Coconut Pie

3 eggs, well beaten
1 cup light corn syrup
¾ cup sugar
2 tablespoons soft butter
  or margarine

1 teaspoon vanilla
⅛ teaspoon salt
1 cup peanuts
½ cup flaked coconut
1 9-inch unbaked pie shell

Combine all ingredients except pie shell. Mix well and turn into pie shell. Bake in a moderately hot oven (375° F) 35 to 45 minutes or until a knife inserted in the center comes out clean. Makes one 9-inch pie.

Quick Coconut Pie

1 cup flaked coconut
2 tablespoons butter
1 package butterscotch
  pudding mix

1¾ cups milk
1 8-inch baked pie shell
3 tablespoons brown sugar
1½ tablespoons light cream

Combine coconut and butter in a saucepan. Cook over medium heat until coconut is golden brown, stirring constantly. Remove half the coconut from saucepan and reserve. Add pudding mix and milk to coconut in saucepan and cook over medium heat until mixture comes to a full boil, stirring constantly. Remove from heat. Cool about 5 minutes, stirring once or twice. Pour into pie shell and cool about 1 hour. Combine reserved coconut with brown sugar and cream. Spread carefully over cooled pie. Bake in a hot oven (425° F) 15 minutes, or until top is bubbly. Serve either warm or cold. Makes one 8-inch pie.

Baked Ice Cream Pie In Cocoa Crust

⅓ cup shortening
1 cup sifted flour
¼ teaspoon salt
4 teaspoons cocoa
4 teaspoons sugar
¾ teaspoon vanilla
3 tablespoons water

1 quart peppermint or
   vanilla ice cream
3 egg whites
¼ teaspoon salt
¾ teaspoon cream of tartar
6 tablespoons sugar
1 teaspoon vanilla

Cut shortening into sifted dry ingredients until mixture is consistency of corn meal and small peas. Combine vanilla and water. Gradually sprinkle enough liquid over flour mixture to dampen dough. Blend with fork or pastry blender. Place dough on waxed paper. Knead 3 times. Let stand at room temperature for 15 to 20 minutes. Roll out dough. Fit into pie pan. Flute edge. Prick pastry. Bake in a very hot oven (450°F.) 8 to 10 minutes. Cool. Pack ice cream firmly into thoroughly cooled pie crust. Wrap, mark and place in freezer if pie is not to be served immediately. Just before serving make meringue by beating egg whites with salt until definite peaks will form when beater is lifted. Gradually beat in cream of tartar and sugar until meringue is very stiff. Add vanilla. Pile meringue lightly over ice cream making sure meringue touches pie crust all the way around. Bake in a very hot oven (450°F.) 3 minutes, or until meringue is delicately browned. Serve immediately. Makes 8 inch deep pie or 9 inch shallow pie.

Swift & Co.

National Biscuit Company

Graham Cracker Cream Pie

1 packet of graham
  crackers, finely rolled
  (1⅔ cups crumbs)
¼ cup butter or margarine,
  softened
¾ cup sugar, divided

3 cups milk
2 packages vanilla
  pudding and pie filling
  mix
4 eggs, separated

Thoroughly blend crumbs with softened butter or margarine and ¼ cup sugar. Pour into a 9-inch pie plate and press firmly against bottom and sides of pie plate. (The easy way is to use an 8-inch pie plate.) Bake in a moderate oven (375°F.) for 7 minutes. Cool.

In a saucepan gradually add milk to pudding and pie filling mix. Stir in beaten egg yolks. Cook over medium heat, stirring constantly until pudding thickens. Cool. Pour into baked crust. Beat egg whites until foamy. Gradually add remaining sugar. Continue beating until stiff. Pile meringue over filling sealing to edges of crust. Bake in a hot oven (425°F.) 4 to 5 minutes, or until lightly browned. Chill 3 to 4 hours. Makes 6 to 8 servings.

Dutch Cottage Cheese Pie

1½ cups creamed cottage
   cheese
3 eggs
1¼ teaspoons salt
3 tablespoons molasses
¼ teaspoon ground
   cinnamon

½ cup dark brown sugar
1 teaspoon lemon juice
¼ cup heavy cream
4 tablespoons flour
6 well-drained canned
   peach halves
1 unbaked 9-inch pie shell

Sieve or beat cottage cheese until smooth. Add and thoroughly beat in eggs one at a time. Blend in salt, molasses, cinnamon, sugar, lemon juice and cream. Sprinkle half of the flour over the cut sides of the peach halves. Add remaining flour to cottage cheese mixture and mix until smooth.

Place floured peach halves, cut side down, in bottom of pie shell, allowing a whole half for each pie serving. Pour in cottage cheese filling carefully. Bake pie in a moderate oven (350°F.), about 50 minutes or until a silver knife inserted in the center comes out clean. Cool before serving. Makes 6 servings.

Sealtest Consumer Service

Apple Butter Pumpkin Pie

1 cup apple butter
1 cup cooked or canned
   mashed pumpkin
½ cup brown sugar,
   firmly packed
½ teaspoon salt

¾ teaspoon cinnamon
¾ teaspoon nutmeg
⅛ teaspoon ginger
3 eggs
¾ cup evaporated milk
1 9-inch unbaked pie shell

Combine apple butter, pumpkin, brown sugar, salt, cinnamon, nutmeg and ginger. Beat eggs and stir into mixture. Gradually add evaporated milk and mix thoroughly. Pour into pie shell. Bake in a hot oven (425° F) 40 to 45 minutes or until a knife inserted in pie comes out clean. Makes one 9-inch pie.

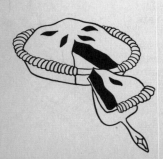

Squash Pie

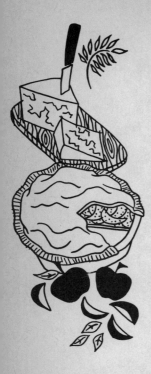

1½ cups cooked,
  strained squash
1 cup brown sugar,
  firmly packed
½ teaspoon salt
2 teaspoons cinnamon

1 teaspoon ginger
2 tablespoons molasses
3 eggs, slightly beaten
1 cup evaporated milk
1 9-inch unbaked pie shell

Mix squash, sugar, salt, spices and molasses. Add eggs and milk and mix thoroughly. Pour mixture into unbaked pie shell. Bake in a hot oven (425° F) 40 to 45 minutes or until a knife inserted in the center comes out clean. Makes one 9-inch pie.

Refrigerator Cheese Pie

20 graham crackers
¼ cup sugar
¼ cup softened butter or
  margarine
1 envelope unflavored
  gelatine
¼ cup cold water
1 egg, separated
¼ cup milk

½ cup sugar
1 cup cottage cheese
1 3-ounce package cream
  cheese
Grated rind of ½ lemon
½ teaspoon vanilla
½ cup light cream
Juice of ½ lemon

Place crackers in a bag and crush fine with a rolling pin. Combine with ¼ cup sugar and softened butter and mix well. Put crumbs in a refrigerator ice cube tray. Press firmly against bottom and sides of tray with a cup. Soften gelatine in cold water. Combine slightly beaten egg yolk, milk and ½ cup sugar; cook over low heat for 5 minutes, stirring constantly. Remove from heat; add gelatine and stir until dissolved. Blend cheeses together; add lemon rind and vanilla. Add gelatine mixture and blend well. Chill until mixture begins to thicken. Beat cream until foamy; add lemon juice and whip until thickened. Beat egg white until stiff. Fold cream and egg white into cheese mixture. Pour into crumb lined refrigerator tray. Chill until firm. Cut into pie shaped wedges for serving. Makes 6 servings.

INDEX